SAINT PAUL

Cultural Memory
in
the
Present

Mieke Bal and Hent de Vries, Editors

SAINT PAUL

The Foundation of Universalism

Alain Badiou

Translated by Ray Brassier

STANFORD UNIVERSITY PRESS

STANFORD, CALIFORNIA

Stanford University Press
Stanford, California
www.sup.org

Originally published as *Saint Paul: La fondation de l'universalisme*, © 1997 by Presses Universitaires de France

Assistance for the translation was provided by the French Ministry of Culture.

Printed in the United States of America on acid-free, archival-quality paper.

Library of Congress Cataloging-in-Publication Data
Badiou, Alain.
    [Saint Paul. English]
    Saint Paul : the foundation of universalism / Alain Badiou; translated by Ray Brassier.
        p. cm.—(Cultural memory in the present)
    ISBN 0-8047-4470-X (cloth : alk. paper)—ISBN 0-8047-4471-8 (alk. paper)
    1. Paul, the Apostle, Saint.   2. Bible N.T. Epistles of Paul—Criticism, inter-
pretation, etc.   3. Universalism—Biblical teaching.   I. Title.   II. Series.
BS2650.52.B3313 2003
225.9'2—dc21   2002154091

Original printing 2003
Last figure below indicates year of this printing:
12   11   10   09   08   07   06   05   04   03

Designed and typeset at Stanford University Press in 11/13.5 Garamond

Contents

Translator's Note

In rendering quotations from Paul into English, I consulted the Authorized, Revised Standard, and New Revised Standard Versions of his epistles. Since my aim was to stick as closely as possible to Badiou's own French rendition, I found the best results were obtained through a selective combination of the Authorized and Revised Standard Versions. I altered or adjusted formulations from both whenever necessary. I translated the quotations from Pascal's *Pensées* in Chapter 4 myself. For the Nietzsche quotations in Chapters 5 and 6, I used R. J. Hollingdale's translation of *The Anti-Christ* (Harmondsworth, Middlesex: Penguin, 1990). These were slightly altered to fit the French version used by Badiou.

This is a book principally concerned with using Paul to redefine the philosophical category of "the subject" as a "universal singularity." Given this putative universality, many readers will balk at the persistent use of the masculine pronoun "he" to refer to this newly defined "subject." Although *sujet* in French is a masculine noun for which the corresponding masculine pronoun *il* (which means both "he" and "it") is habitually substituted, it has become customary in English translations of contemporary French philosophical texts to correct this gender bias by stipulating "he or she" (or "it") whenever the French has *il* standing in for a term like *sujet*. However, in the context of the present work, two considerations rendered this customary tactic particularly problematic: the first, practical and stylistic; the second, substantive and thematic. First, from a purely practical point of view, there were too many sentences in which the concatenation of abstract nouns meant that using the pronoun "it" to refer to "the subject" would have created ambiguity at best, unacceptable confusion at worst. In addition, there were equally many instances in which substituting "he or she" for "it" would have destroyed the rhythm, poise, and symmetry of Badiou's meticulously constructed sentences. Although such practical and stylistic considerations invited a disinterested choice between the consistent use of either "he" or "she," it was the second, more substantive and thematic point of view that seemed to render the use of the masculine pronoun appropriate and that finally persuaded me to opt for "he." I refer here to Badiou's explicit comments throughout Chapters 4, 5, and 6 about the "filiation" of the Pauline subject, a filiation necessitating the latter's unequivocal characterization as a Son (in French, *filiation* already contains the word *fils*, "son").

I would like to thank Alberto Toscano and Peter Hallward for their friendly but indispensable advice.

RAY BRASSIER

SAINT PAUL

Prologue

Strange enterprise. For a long time, this figure has accompanied me, along with others: Mallarmé, Cantor, Archimedes, Plato, Robespierre, Conrad . . . (and this is without venturing into our own century). Fifteen years ago, I wrote a play, *The Incident at Antioch*, whose heroine was named Paula. The change of sex probably prevented too explicit an identification. For me, truth be told, Paul is not an apostle or a saint. I care nothing for the Good News he declares, or the cult dedicated to him. But he is a subjective figure of primary importance. I have always read the epistles the way one returns to those classic texts with which one is particularly familiar; their paths well worn, their details abolished, their power preserved. No transcendence, nothing sacred, perfect equality of this work with every other, the moment it touches me personally. A man emphatically inscribed these phrases, these vehement and tender addresses, and we may draw upon them freely, without devotion or repulsion. All the more so in my case, since, irreligious by heredity, and even encouraged in the desire to crush the clerical infamy by my four grandparents, all of whom were teachers, I encountered the epistles late, the way one encounters curious texts whose poetry astonishes.

Basically, I have never really connected Paul with religion. It is not according to this register, or to bear witness to any sort of faith, or even antifaith, that I have, for a long time, been interested in him. No more so, to tell the truth—but the impression was less striking—than I seized hold of Pascal, Kierkegaard, or Claudel, on the basis of what was explicitly Christian in their discourse. Anyway, the crucible in which what will become a work of art and thought burns is brimful with nameless impurities; it comprises obsessions, beliefs, infantile puzzles, various perversions, undivulgeable memories, haphazard reading, and quite a few idiocies and chimeras. Analyzing this alchemy is of little use.

For me, Paul is a poet-thinker of the event, as well as one who practices and states the invariant traits of what can be called the militant figure. He brings forth the entirely human connection, whose destiny fascinates me, between the general idea of a rupture, an overturning, and that of a thought-practice that is this rupture's subjective materiality.

If today I wish to retrace in a few pages the singularity of this connection in Paul, it is probably because there is currently a widespread search for a new militant figure—even if it takes the form of denying its possibility—called upon to succeed the one installed by Lenin and the Bolsheviks at the beginning of the century, which can be said to have been that of the party militant.

When a step forward is the order of the day, one may, among other things, find assistance in the greatest step back. Whence this reactivation of Paul. I am not the first to risk the comparison that makes of him a Lenin for whom Christ will have been the equivocal Marx.

My intention, clearly, is neither historicizing nor exegetical. It is subjective through and through. I have confined myself strictly to those texts of Paul that have been authenticated by contemporary scholarship and to the relation they bear to my thought.

For the Greek original, I used the *Novum Testamentum Graece*, in Nestlé-Aland's critical edition, published by Deutsche Bibelgesellschaft in 1993.

The basic French text, whose formulations I have sometimes altered, is that by Louis Segond, *Le Nouveau Testament*, published by the Trinitarian Bible Society (1993 edition).

References to the epistles follow the customary arrangement by chapter and verse. Thus, Rom. 1.25 means: epistle to the Romans, chapter 1, verse 25. Similarly, we will say Gal. for the epistle to the Galatians, Cor. I and Cor. II for the two epistles to the Corinthians, Philipp. for the epistle to the Philippians, and Thess. I for the first epistle to the Thessa-lonians.

For anyone interested in further reading, I would at least like to in-dicate two works from among the colossal secondary literature on Paul:

Stanislas Breton's robust little book, *Saint Paul* (Paris: Presses Uni-versitaire de France, 2000).

Günther Bornkamm's *Paul*, translated by D.M.G. Stalker (Min-neapolis: Fortress Press, 1995).

A Catholic, a Protestant. May they form a triangle with the atheist.

1

Paul: Our Contemporary

Why Saint Paul? Why solicit this "apostle" who is all the more suspect for having, it seems, proclaimed himself such and whose name is frequently tied to Christianity's least open, most institutional aspects: the Church, moral discipline, social conservatism, suspiciousness toward Jews? How are we to inscribe this name into the development of our project: to refound a theory of the Subject that subordinates its existence to the aleatory dimension of the event as well as to the pure contingency of multiple-being without sacrificing the theme of freedom?

Similarly, one will ask: What use do we claim to make of the apparatus of Christian faith, an apparatus from which it seems strictly impossible to dissociate the figure and texts of Paul? Why invoke and analyze this fable? Let us be perfectly clear: so far as we are concerned, what we are dealing with here is precisely a fable. And singularly so in the case of Paul, who for crucial reasons reduces Christianity to a single statement: Jesus is resurrected. Yet this is precisely a fabulous element [*point fabuleux*], since all the rest, birth, teachings, death, *might* after all be upheld. A "fable" is that part of a narrative that, so far as we are concerned, fails to touch on any Real, unless it be by virtue of that invisible and indirectly accessible residue sticking to every obvious imaginary. In this regard, it is to its element of fabulation [*point de fable*] alone that Paul reduces the Christian narrative, with the strength of one who knows that in holding fast to this point as real, one is unburdened of all the imaginary that surrounds it. If it is possible for us to speak of belief from the outset (but Paul's entire problem concerns the question of belief or faith, or of that which is presupposed beneath the word *pistis*), let us say that so far as we are concerned it is rigorously impossible to believe in the resurrection of the crucified.

Paul is a distant figure in a threefold sense: his historical site; his role as Church founder; and his provocative centering of thought upon its fabulous element.

We are duty-bound to explain why we are investing this distance with the weight of a philosophical proximity, why the fabulous forcing of the real provides us with mediation when it is a question of restoring the universal to its pure secularity, here and now.

We are doubtless assisted in this by the fact that—for example—Hegel, Auguste Comte, Nietzsche, Freud, Heidegger, and again in our own time, Jean-François Lyotard, have also found it necessary to examine the figure of Paul and have done so, moreover, always in terms of some extreme dispositions (foundational or regressive, destinal or forgetful, exemplary or catastrophic) in order to organize their own speculative discourses.

For our own part, what we shall focus on in Paul's work is a singular connection, which it is formally possible to disjoin from the fable and of which Paul is, strictly speaking, the inventor: the connection that establishes a passage between a proposition concerning the subject and an interrogation concerning the law. Let us say that, for Paul, it is a matter of investigating which law is capable of structuring a subject devoid of all identity and suspended to an event whose only "proof" lies precisely in its having been declared by a subject.

What is essential for us is that this paradoxical connection between a subject without identity and a law without support provides the foundation for the possibility of a universal teaching within history itself. Paul's unprecedented gesture consists in subtracting truth from the communitarian grasp, be it that of a people, a city, an empire, a territory, or a social class. What is true (or just; they are the same in this case) cannot be reduced to any objective aggregate, either by its cause or by its destination.

It will be objected that, in the present case, for us "truth" designates a mere fable. Granted, but what is important is the subjective gesture grasped in its founding power with respect to the generic conditions of universality. That the content of the fable must be abandoned leaves as its remainder the form of these conditions and, in particular, the ruin of every attempt to assign the discourse of truth to preconstituted historical aggregates.

To sharply separate each truth procedure from the cultural "historicity" wherein opinion presumes to dissolve it: such is the operation in which Paul is our guide.

To rethink this gesture, to unravel its twists and turns, to enliven its singularity, its instituting force, is without doubt a contemporary necessity.

What, in effect, does our contemporary situation consist of? The progressive reduction of the question of truth (and hence, of thought) to a linguistic form, judgment—a point on which Anglophone analytical ideology and the hermeneutical tradition both concur (the analytic/ hermeneutic doublet is the straightjacket of contemporary academic philosophy)—ends up in a cultural and historical relativism that today constitutes at once a topic of public opinion, a "political" motivation, and a framework for research in the human sciences. The extreme forms of this relativism, already at work, claim to relegate mathematics itself to an "Occidental" setup, to which any number of obscurantist or symbolically trivial apparatuses could be rendered equivalent, provided one is able to name the subset of humanity that supports this apparatus, and, better still, that one has reasons for believing this subset to be made up of victims. All access to the universal, which neither tolerates assignation to the particular, nor maintains any direct relation with the status— whether it be that of dominator or victim—of the *sites* from which its proposition emerges, collapses when confronted with this intersection between culturalist ideology and the "victimist" [*victimaire*] conception of man.

What is the real unifying factor behind this attempt to promote the cultural virtue of oppressed subsets, this invocation of language in order to extol communitarian particularisms (which, besides language, always ultimately refer back to race, religion, or gender)? It is, evidently, monetary abstraction, whose false universality has absolutely no difficulty accommodating the kaleidoscope of communitarianisms. The lengthy years of communist dictatorship will have had the merit of showing that financial globalization, the absolute sovereignty of capital's empty universality, had as its only genuine enemy another universal project, albeit a corrupt and bloodstained one: that only Lenin and Mao truly *frightened* those who proposed to boast unreservedly about the merits of liberalism and the general equivalent, or the democratic virtues of commercial communication. The senescent collapse of the USSR, the paradigm of socialist States, provisionally suspended fear, unleashed empty abstraction, debased thought in general. And it is certainly not by renouncing the concrete universality of truths in order to affirm the rights of "minorities," be they racial, religious, national, or sexual, that the devastation will be slowed down. No, we will not allow the rights of true-thought to have as their only instance monetarist free exchange and its mediocre political appendage, capitalist-parliamentarianism, whose squalor is ever more poorly dissimulated behind the fine word "democracy."

This is why Paul, himself the contemporary of a monumental figure of the destruction of all politics (the beginnings of that military despotism known as "the Roman Empire"), interests us in the highest degree. He is the one who, assigning to the universal a specific connection of law and the subject, asks himself with the most extreme rigor what price is to be paid for this assignment, by the law as well as by the subject. This interrogation is precisely our own. Supposing we were able to refound the connection between truth and the subject, then what consequences must we have the strength to hold fast to, on the side of truth (eventual [*événementielle*] and hazardous) as well as on the side of the subject (rare and heroic)?

It is by confronting this question, and no other, that philosophy can assume its temporal condition without becoming a means of covering up the worst. That it can measure up to the times in which we live otherwise than by flattering their savage inertia.

In the case of our own country, France, of the public destiny of its State, what can we point to in the way of a noticeable tendency of the last fifteen years? Notwithstanding, of course, the constant expansion of capital's automatic functioning that shelters behind the signifiers of Europe and liberalism, an expansion that, being the law of the world-market, cannot be taken as specific to our site.

Alas, the only thing we can point to by way of reply to this question is the permanent installation of Le Pen's party,* a truly national singularity, whose equivalent we have to go all the way to Austria to find, hardly a flattering comparison. And what constitutes this party's unique maxim? The maxim that none of the parliamentary parties dare directly oppose, so that they all vote for or tolerate those increasingly villainous laws that are implacably deduced from it? The maxim in question is: "France for the French." In the case of the State, this leads back to what served as the paradoxical name given by Pétain to a puppet state, zealous servant of the Nazi occupier: the French State. How does the noxious question "What is a French person?" come to install itself at the heart of the public sphere? But everyone knows there is no tenable answer to this question other than through the persecution of those people arbitrarily designated as the non-French. The unique *political* real proper to the word "French," when the latter is upheld as a founding category in the State, is the increasingly insistent installation of relentlessly discriminatory measures targeting people who are here, or who are trying to live here. And it is particularly striking that this persecutory real proper to identitarian logic (the Law is only valid *for the French*) gathers under the same banner—as is shown by the sorry affair of the *foulard***—resigned advocates of capitalist devastation (persecution is inevitable because unemployment precludes all hospitality) and advocates of a "French republic" as ghostly as it is exceptional (foreigners are only tolerable so long as they "integrate" themselves into the magnificent model presented to them by our pure in-

*A reference to Jean-Marie Le Pen's *Front National,* an extreme right-wing party that continues to enjoy significant electoral success in France.—Trans.

** *L'affaire du foulard* refers to a controversy over the wearing of the traditional Muslim headscarf (*foulard*) by young Arab women in French secondary schools. Since the French educational system explicitly prohibits the wearing of religious garb or paraphernalia in class, some teachers protested and refused to teach students who insisted on wearing the headscarf, arguing that tolerating the infraction of one ethnic group provided a dangerous precedent that could only incite students of other religious denominations to follow suit, thereby undermining the French educational system's secular ethos.—Trans.

stitutions, our astonishing systems of education and representation). Proof that, so far as peoples' real lives and what happens to them is concerned, there exists a despicable complicity between the globalized logic of capital and French identitarian fanaticism.

What is being constructed before our very eyes is the communitarization of the public sphere, the renunciation of the law's transcendent neutrality. The State is supposed to assure itself primarily and permanently of the genealogically, religiously, and racially verifiable identity of those for whom it is responsible. It is required to define two, perhaps even three, distinct regions of the law, according to whether the latter are truly French, integrated or integratable foreigners, or finally foreigners who are declared to be unintegrated, or even unintegratable. The law thereby falls under the control of a "national" model devoid of any real principle, unless it be that of the persecutions it initiates. Abandoning all universal principle, identitarian verification—which is never anything but police monitoring—comes to take precedence over the definition or application of the law. This means that, just as under Pétain, when ministers saw nothing wrong in surreptitiously defining the Jew as prototype of the non-French, all legislation would be accompanied by the required identitarian protocols, and subsets of the population would come to be defined each time by their *special status*. This arrangement is taking its course, as successive governments each bring to it their own special touch. We are dealing with a rampant "Pétainization" of the State.

How clearly Paul's statement rings out under these conditions! A genuinely stupefying statement when one knows the rules of the ancient world: "There is neither Jew nor Greek, there is neither slave nor free, there is neither male nor female" (Gal. 3.28)! And how appropriate, for we who will unproblematically replace God by this or that truth, and Good by the service this truth requires, the maxim "Glory, honor, and peace for every one that does good, to the Jew first and also to the Greek. For God shows no partiality" (Rom. 2.10).

Our world is in no way as "complex" as those who wish to ensure its perpetuation claim. It is even, in its broad outline, perfectly simple.

On the one hand, there is an extension of the automatisms of capital, fulfilling one of Marx's inspired predictions: the world finally *configured*, but as a market, as a world-market. This configuration imposes the rule of an abstract homogenization. Everything that circulates falls under the unity of a count, while inversely, only what lets itself be counted in this way can circulate. Moreover, this is the norm that illuminates a paradox few have pointed out: in the hour of generalized circulation and the phantasm of instantaneous cultural communication, laws and regulations forbidding the circulation of persons are being multiplied everywhere. So it is that in France, never have fewer foreigners settled than in the recent period! Free circulation of what lets itself be counted, yes, and above all of capital, which is the count of the count. Free circulation of that uncountable infinity constituted by a singular human life, never! For capitalist monetary abstraction is certainly a singularity, but a singularity *that has no consideration for any singularity whatsoever*: singularity as indifferent to the persistent infinity of existence as it is to the evental becoming of truths.

On the other side, there is a process of fragmentation into closed identities, and the culturalist and relativist ideology that accompanies this fragmentation.

Both processes are perfectly intertwined. For each identification (the creation or cobbling together of identity) creates a figure that provides a material for its investment by the market. There is nothing more captive, so far as commercial investment is concerned, nothing more *amenable* to the invention of new figures of monetary homogeneity, than a community and its territory or territories. The semblance of a nonequivalence is required so that equivalence itself can constitute a process. What inexhaustible potential for mercantile investments in this upsurge—taking the form of communities demanding recognition and so-called cultural singularities—of women, homosexuals, the disabled, Arabs! And these infinite combinations of predicative traits, what a godsend! Black homosexuals, disabled Serbs, Catholic pedophiles, moderate Muslims, married priests, ecologist yuppies, the submissive unemployed, prematurely aged youth! Each time, a social image authorizes new products, specialized magazines, improved shopping malls, "free" radio stations, targeted advertising networks, and finally, heady "public debates" at peak viewing times. Deleuze put it perfectly: capitalist deterritorialization requires a constant reterritorialization. Capital demands a permanent creation of subjective and territorial identities in order for its prin-

ciple of movement to homogenize its space of action; identities, moreover, that never demand anything but the right to be exposed in the same
way as others to the uniform prerogatives of the market. The capitalist
logic of the general equivalent and the identitarian and cultural logic of
communities or minorities form an articulated whole.

This articulation plays a constraining role relative to every truth
procedure. It is organically *without truth*.

On the one hand, every truth procedure breaks with the axiomatic
principle that governs the situation and organizes its repetitive series. A
truth procedure interrupts repetition and can therefore not be supported
by the abstract permanence proper to a unity of the count. A truth is always, according to the dominant law of the count, subtracted from the
count. Consequently, no truth can be sustained through capital's homogeneous expansion.

But, on the other hand, neither can a truth procedure take root in
the element of identity. For if it is true that every truth erupts as singular,
its singularity is immediately universalizable. Universalizable singularity
necessarily breaks with identitarian singularity.

That there are intertwined histories, different cultures and, more
generally, differences already abundant in one and the "same" individual,
that the world is multicolored, that one must let people live, eat, dress,
imagine, love in whichever way they please, is not the issue, whatever certain disingenuous simpletons may want us to think. Such liberal truisms
are cheap, and one would only like to see those who proclaim them not
react so violently whenever confronted with the slightest serious attempt
to dissent from their own puny liberal difference. Contemporary cosmopolitanism is a beneficent reality. We simply ask that its partisans not
get themselves worked up at the sight of a young veiled woman, lest we
begin to fear that what they really desire, far from a real web of shifting
differences, is the uniform dictatorship of what they take to be "modernity."

It is a question of knowing what identitarian and communitarian
categories have to do with truth procedures, with political procedures for
example. We reply: these categories must be *absented* from the process,
failing which no truth has the slightest chance of establishing its persistence and accruing its immanent infinity. We know, moreover, that the

most consequential instances of identitarian politics, such as Nazism, are bellicose and criminal. The idea that one can wield such categories innocently, even in the form of French "republican" identity, is inconsistent. One will, of necessity, end up oscillating between the abstract universal of capital and localized persecutions.

The contemporary world is thus doubly hostile to truth procedures. This hostility betrays itself though nominal occlusions: where the name of a truth procedure should obtain, another, which represses it, holds sway. The name "culture" comes to obliterate that of "art." The word "technology" obliterates the word "science." The word "management" obliterates the word "politics." The word "sexuality" obliterates love. The "culture-technology-management-sexuality" system, which has the immense merit of being homogeneous to the market, and all of whose terms designate a category of commercial presentation, constitutes the modern nominal occlusion of the "art-science-politics-love" system, which identifies truth procedures typologically.

Now, far from returning toward an appropriation of this typology, identitarian or minoritarian logic merely proposes a variant on its nominal occlusion by capital. It inveighs against every generic concept of art, putting the concept of culture in its place, conceived as culture of the group, as the subjective or representative glue for the group's existence, a culture that addresses only itself and remains potentially nonuniversalizable. Moreover, it does not hesitate to posit that this culture's constitutive elements are only fully comprehensible on the condition that one belong to the subset in question. Whence catastrophic pronouncements of the sort: only a homosexual can "understand" what a homosexual is, only an Arab can understand what an Arab is, and so forth. If, as we believe, only truths (thought) allow man to be distinguished from the human animal that underlies him, it is no exaggeration to say that such minoritarian pronouncements are genuinely *barbaric*. In the case of science, culturalism promotes the technical particularity of subsets to the equivalent of scientific thought, so that antibiotics, Shamanism, the laying on of hands, or emollient herbal teas all become of equal worth. In the case of politics, the consideration of identitarian traits provides the basis for determination, be it the state's or the protestor's, and finally it is a matter of stipulating, through law or brute force, an authoritarian management of these traits (national, religious, sexual, and so on) considered as dominant political operators. Lastly, in the case of love, there will be the complementary demands, either for the genetic right to have such and such a form of specialized sexual behavior recognized as a minoritarian identity; or for the return, pure and simple, to archaic, culturally established conceptions, such as that of strict conjugality, the confinement of women, and so forth. It is perfectly possible to combine the two, as becomes apparent when homosexual protest concerns the right to be reincluded in the grand traditionalism of marriage and the family, or to take responsibility for the defrocking of a priest with the Pope's blessing.

The two components of the articulated whole (abstract homogeneity of capital and identitarian protest) are in a relation of reciprocal maintenance and mirroring. Who will maintain the self-evident superiority of the competent–cultivated–sexually liberated manager? But who will defend the corrupt-religious–polygamist terrorist? Or eulogize the cultural-marginal–homeopathic–media-friendly transsexual? Each figure gains its rotating legitimacy from the other's discredit. Yet at the same time, each draws on the resources of the other, since the transformation of the most typical, most recent communitarian identities into advertising selling points and salable images has for its counterpart the ever more refined competence that the most insular or most violent groups display when it comes to speculating on the financial markets or maintaining a large-scale arms commerce.

Breaking with all this (neither monetary homogeneity nor identitarian protest; neither the abstract universality of capital nor the particularity of interests proper to a subset), our question can be clearly formulated: What are the conditions for a *universal singularity*?

It is on this point that we invoke Saint Paul, for this is precisely his question. What does Paul want? Probably to drag the Good News (the Gospels) out from the rigid enclosure within which its restriction to the Jewish community would confine it. But equally, never to let it be determined by the available generalities, be they statist [*étatiques*] or ideological. Statist generality belongs to Roman legalism, and to Roman citizenship in particular, to its conditions and the rights associated with it. Although himself a Roman citizen, and proud of it, Paul will never allow any legal categories to identify the Christian subject. Slaves, women, people of every profession and nationality will therefore be admitted without restriction or privilege. As for ideological generality, it is obviously represented by the philosophical and moral discourse of the Greeks. Paul will establish a resolute distance to this discourse, which is for him the counterpoise to a conservative vision of Jewish law. Ultimately, it is a case of mobilizing a universal singularity both against the prevailing abstractions (legal then, economic now), and against communitarian or particularist protest.

Paul's general procedure is the following: if there has been an event, and if truth consists in declaring it and then in being faithful to this declaration, two consequences ensue. First, since truth is eventual, or of the order of what occurs, it is singular. It is neither structural, nor axiomatic, nor legal. No available generality can account for it, nor structure the subject who claims to follow in its wake. Consequently, there cannot be a law of truth. Second, truth being inscribed on the basis of a declaration that is in essence subjective, no preconstituted subset can support it; nothing communitarian or historically established can lend its substance to the process of truth. Truth is diagonal relative to every communitarian subset; it neither claims authority from, nor (this is obviously the most delicate point) constitutes any identity. It is offered to all, or addressed to everyone, without a condition of belonging being able to limit this offer, or this address.

Once the texts transmitted to us are all seen as local interventions, and hence governed by localized tactical stakes, Paul's problematic, however sinewy its articulation, implacably follows the requirements of truth as universal singularity:

1. The Christian subject does not preexist the event he declares (Christ's resurrection). Thus, the extrinsic conditions of his existence or identity will be argued against. He will be required to be neither Jewish (or circumcised), nor Greek (or wise). This is the theory of discourses (there are three: the Jewish, the Greek, the new). No more than he will be required to be from this or that social class (theory of equality before truth), or this or that sex (theory of women).

2. Truth is entirely subjective (it is of the order of a declaration that testifies to a conviction relative to the event). Thus, every sub-

sumption of its becoming under a law will be argued against. It will be necessary to proceed at once via a radical critique of Jewish law, which has become obsolete and harmful, and of Greek law as the subordination of destiny to the cosmic order, which has never been anything but a "learned" ignorance of the paths of salvation.

3. Fidelity to the declaration is crucial, for truth is a process, and not an illumination. In order to think it, one requires three concepts: one that names the subject at the point of declaration (*pistis*, generally translated as "faith," but which is more appropriately rendered as "conviction"); one that names the subject at the point of his conviction's militant address (*agapē*, generally translated as "charity," but more appropriately rendered as "love"); lastly, one that names the subject according to the force of displacement conferred upon him through the assumption of the truth procedure's *completed* [*achevé*] character (*elpis*, generally translated as "hope," but more appropriately rendered as "certainty").

4. A truth is of itself indifferent to the state of the situation, to the Roman State for example. This means that it is subtracted from the organization of subsets prescribed by that state. The subjectivity corresponding to this subtraction constitutes a necessary *distance* from the State and from what corresponds to the State in people's consciousness: the apparatus of opinion. One must not argue about opinions, Paul says. A truth is a concentrated and serious procedure, which must never enter into competition with established opinions.

There is not one of these maxims which, setting aside the content of the event, cannot be appropriated for our situation and our philosophical tasks. All that remains is to deploy their underlying conceptual organization, while giving credit to him who, deciding that none was exempt from what a truth demands and disjoining the true from the Law, provoked—entirely alone—a cultural revolution upon which we still depend.

2

Who Is Paul?

We could begin in the sanctimonious style of the usual biographies. Paul (actually Saul, the name of the first king of Israel) is born in Tarsus between 1 and 5 A.D. (impossible, from a strictly scholarly perspective, to be more precise). Thus, he is of the same generation as Jesus, who, as everyone knows—but the circularity is interesting—is born and concurrently establishes his own date of birth by instituting year 1 of "our" era ("his," rather). Paul's father is an artisan-retailer, a tent maker. He is a Roman citizen, and hence so is Paul. How did this father obtain citizenship? It is simplest to suppose, despite the absence of evidence, that he bought it. It would not be beyond the means of an affluent retailer to bribe a Roman civil servant. Paul is a Jew of the Pharisaical tendency. He is an ardent participant in the persecution of Christians, who are considered heretics by the orthodox Jews and, as a result, legally prosecuted but also beaten, stoned, and driven out, in accordance with the varying power struggles between different factions in the Jewish communities.

Christ's execution dates approximately from the year 30. We are in the reign of Tiberius. In the year 33 or 34, on the road to Damascus Paul is struck by a divine apparition and converts to Christianity. He begins his famous missionary voyages. And so on.

What use is all this? You can consult the books. Let's cut straight to the doctrine.

And yet, no, let us pause instead. Paul is a major figure of antiphilosophy. But it is of the essence of antiphilosophy that the subjective position figure as a decisive factor in discourse. Existential fragments, sometimes anecdotal in appearance, are elevated to the rank of guarantor of truth. Can one imagine Rousseau without the *Confessions*, Kierkegaard without our being informed of the detail of his engagement to Regine, or Nietzsche not inviting us to pay witness, throughout *Ecce Homo*, to the reasons entitling him to ask the question "Why am I a destiny"? For an antiphilosopher, the enunciative position is obviously part of the statement's protocol. No discourse can lay claim to truth if it does not contain an explicit answer to the question: Who speaks?

Whenever Paul addresses his writings, he always draws attention to the fact that he has been entitled to speak as a subject. And he *became* this subject. He became it suddenly, on the road to Damascus (if, as we believe, in this particular instance one can, for once and once only, trust that fabricated biography of Paul that the New Testament presents under the title Acts of the Apostles). The story is well known: while traveling to Damascus as a zealous Pharisee in order to persecute Christians, Paul hears a mysterious voice revealing to him both the truth and his vocation.

Is the term "conversion" appropriate to what happened on the road to Damascus? It was a thunderbolt, a caesura, and not a dialectical reversal. It was a conscription instituting a new subject: "By the grace of God I am what I am [*eimi ho eimi*]" (Cor. I.15.10). What this absolutely aleatory intervention on the road to Damascus summons is the "I am" as such.

In a certain sense, this conversion isn't carried out by anyone: Paul has not been converted by representatives of "the Church"; he has not been won over. He has not been presented with the gospel. Clearly, the encounter on the road mimics the founding event. Just as the Resurrection remains totally incalculable and it is from there that one must begin, Paul's faith is that from which he begins as a subject, and nothing leads up to it. The event—"it happened," purely and simply, in the anonymity of a road—is the subjective sign of the event proper that is the Resurrection of Christ. Within Paul himself, it is the (re)surgence [*(ré)surrection*] of the subject. This is the exemplary matrix of the link between existence and doctrine, for Paul draws from the conditions of his "conversion" the consequence that one can only begin from faith, from the declaration of faith. The sudden appearance of the Christian subject is unconditioned.

Accordingly, if we are to grasp his message, we can in no way neglect the circumstances of Paul's life. In this regard, it is fortunate that those circumstances to which we accord the highest importance are the ones he himself incorporates into his epistles. For reliable independent evidence is extremely rare. The narrative of the Acts of the Apostles is, as we have already mentioned, a retrospective construction whose intentions modern criticism has clearly brought to light, and whose form is frequently borrowed from the rhetoric of Greek fables. To distinguish its real elements from the edifying (and politically charged) fable in which they are enveloped requires an exceptional and suspicious rigor. And we have practically nothing else to go on, unless it be the ability to verify such and such a detail through the intermediary of Roman historiography, which couldn't have cared less about these little groups of Jewish heretics. Moreover, one must be suspicious even of "Paul's epistles," canonically gathered together in the New Testament at least a century after the apostle's death. Scholarly exegesis has demonstrated the apocryphal nature of many of them, to the extent that the corpus of this fundamental author must, in the final analysis, be reduced to six rather brief texts: Romans, Corinthians I and II, Galatians, Philippians, and Thessalonians I. This is nonetheless enough to establish certain major subjective traits and guarantee certain decisive episodes.

Thus, for example, a point of the highest importance, which Paul relates to us with noticeable pride (Paul is certainly neither introverted, nor falsely modest): What does he do after the Damascus experience? We know in any case *what he does not do*. He does not go to Jerusalem; he does not go to see the authorities, the institutional apostles, those who knew Christ. He does not seek "confirmation" for the event that appoints him in his own eyes as an apostle. He leaves this subjective upsurge outside every official seal. The unshakable conviction as to his own destiny probably dates from here, a conviction that will on several occasions cause him to come into conflict with the core of historical apostles, among whom Peter is the central figure. Turning away from all authority other than that of the Voice that personally summoned him to his becoming-subject, Paul leaves for Arabia in order to proclaim the gospel, to declare that what took place did take place. A man who, armed with a personal event, has grounds for declaring that impersonal event that is the Resurrection.

Paul stays in Arabia for three years. Doubtless, in his own eyes, his militant efficacy provides a sufficient guarantee, so that having endured this delay he is finally entitled to meet the Church's "historic leaders." We shall see later that although stubborn, even violent, where matters of principle are concerned, Paul is also a politician, one who knows the value of reasonable compromise, and particularly of verbal compromises, which only slightly impede his freedom of action in the places and territories he chooses (preferably those where his opponent has the least footing). Thus, Paul goes to Jerusalem, where he meets Peter and the apostles, then leaves again. We know nothing of the issues debated in this first meeting. It seems it did not convince Paul of the necessity of frequently consulting with the Jerusalemite "center," because his second period of militant voyage will last fourteen years! Cilicia, Syria, Turkey, Macedonia, Greece. The *ex-centered* dimension of Paul's action is the practical substructure of his thought, which posits that all true universality is devoid of a center.

We know roughly how these militant peregrinations functioned. At that time Judaism was still a proselytizing religion. To address oneself to Gentiles was not, as is often thought, an invention of Paul's. Jewish proselytism was substantial and developed. It divided its audience into two circles that could be called, using a risky political anachronism, the sympathizers and the adherents:

(a) The "God-fearing" recognize monotheism's global legitimacy but are exempt from the prescriptions of the law, and notably from circumcision.

(b) The converted are committed to following the prescriptions of the law, and must be circumcised. Circumcision here indexes its function as a form of branding, of primary initiation.

Thus, it is not primarily the fact that he addresses Gentiles that isolates Paul from the Jewish community. Moreover, Paul begins his teaching by basing himself on that community's institutions. When he arrives in a town, he first intervenes in the synagogue. Unsurprisingly, things go badly with the orthodox, for reasons of doctrine: the stubborn persistence in affirming that Jesus *is* the Messiah (remember that "Christ" is simply the Greek word for "messiah," so that the only continuity between the Good News according to Paul and prophetic Judaism is the equation Jesus = Christ), an affirmation that, in the eyes of the majority of Jews, and for extremely powerful and legitimate reasons, propounds a fraud. Following incidents that, in the conditions of the time, could be extremely violent, and where, basically, one risks one's life, Paul abandons the synagogue and withdraws to the home of a local sympathizer. There he tries to set up a group comprising Judeo-Christians and Gentile-Christians. It seems that very quickly the Gentile-Christians will constitute the majority among the adherents of the group. In light of the minimal concession Paul makes to the Jewish heritage, particularly so far as rites are concerned, this is not in the least surprising. Once the group has been sufficiently consolidated in his eyes (it will then be called an *ekklēsia*, from which *église* [church] undoubtedly derives, although the former should be envisioned in terms of a small group of militants), Paul entrusts its running to those whose conviction he holds in high regard, and who will become his lieutenants. Then he continues on his voyage.

Nothing bears witness to Paul's certainty concerning the future of his action so much as the identification, toward which he is constantly proceeding, between a small core of the constituted faithful in a town and the entire region. Who are these Thessalonians, these Corinthians, to say nothing of these Romans, to whom Paul addresses, in an animated and majestic tone, his epistles? Probably a few "brothers"—which is an archaic form of our "comrades"—lost in the city. Through their commensurability with a truth, anonymous individuals are always transformed into vectors of humanity as a whole. Let's just say that the handful of Resistance fighters in the year 1940 or 1941 occupy the same position as Paul's Corinthians: it is to them, and to them alone, that it is legitimate to address oneself if seeking to indicate a real proper to France.

However far away, Paul never loses sight of these enclaves of the faithful whose existence he has played midwife to. His epistles are nothing but interventions in the lives of these enclaves, and these are possessed of all the political passion proper to such interventions. Struggles against internecine divisions, reminders of fundamental principles, reassertions of trust in local organizers, examinations of litigious points, pressing demands for continuing proselytizing activity, organization of finances . . . Nothing that an activist for any organized cause would not recognize as fundamental to the concerns and passions of collective intervention.

After fourteen years of organizational wandering, of which no written trace remains, we are roughly in the year 50. About twenty years have passed since the death of Christ. It has been seventeen years since Paul received the Damascus convocation. He is in his fifties and refers to himself as "the old Paul." His earliest texts that have been handed down to us date from this period. Why? A few hypotheses can be proposed.

Since he is responsible for several groups largely comprised of Gentile-Christians, Paul resides in Antioch, a very large city, the third city of the empire after Rome and Alexandria. Recall that Paul was born into a well-off family in Tarsus, that he is a man of the city rather than a man of the country. This is more than a detail. His style owes nothing to those rural images and metaphors that, on the contrary, abound in the parables of Christ. If his vision of things fervently embraces the dimension of the world and extends to the extreme limits of the empire (his dearest wish is to go to Spain, as if he, the Oriental, could only accomplish his mission at the extreme edge of the Occident), it is because urban cosmopolitanism and lengthy voyages have shaped its amplitude. Paul's universalism also comprises an internal geography, which is not that of the perennial little landowner.

If Paul begins to write about points of doctrine, if his texts are copied and circulated, we believe it is because he becomes aware of the necessity of engaging in a large-scale struggle. The situation forces him to conceive of himself as leader of a party or faction.

During Paul's stay in Antioch, some Judeo-Christians of strict observance arrive. They confront the apostle, sow discord, demand the circumcision of all the faithful. Once again, it is not proselytism toward non-Jews that is in question. The point is that Paul cannot consent to the distinction between two circles among those whom he has rallied, the doctrinal sympathizers and the "true" converts, initiated and circumcised. For him (and we shall grant him this point), a truth procedure does not comprise degrees. Either one participates in it, declaring the founding event and drawing its consequences, or one remains foreign to it. This distinction, without intermediary or mediation, is entirely subjective. Rites and external markings can provide neither a foundation, nor even a qualification for it. Such is the price for truth's status as a universal singularity. A truth procedure is only universal insofar as it is supported, at that point through which it indexes the real, by an immediate subjective recognition of its singularity. Failing which, one resorts to observances or particular signs, which can only *fix* the Good News within the communitarian space, blocking its universal deployment. Thus, Paul considers all converts as fully practicing followers, whatever their background, and regardless of whether they are circumcised. Judeo-Christians of strict observance maintain the practice of distinguishing between degrees of belonging and find it genuinely scandalous that individuals possessing neither the markings nor the ritual practices of the community can be considered as equals. People who, in a word, have neither the slightest knowledge of, nor respect for, the Law.

A grave dispute ensues. It is finally decided that the issue be settled with the historical apostles in Jerusalem. It is Paul's second encounter with Peter, and this time we have information about what was at stake. It concerns a major conflict, one in which the destiny of the new doctrine is at issue. To what extent does the latter remain dependent on its origin in the Jewish community? In my own language: What is the exact relation between the supposed universality of the postevental truth (that is, what is inferred from Christ's resurrection) and the evental site, which is, indubitably, the nation bound together by the Old Testament? Of what import are the traditional marks of belonging to the Jewish community for the construction of this truth, for its deployment in the peoples of the empire?

The Jerusalem conference (in 50? in 51?) is of decisive importance for these questions, which coordinate the binding of singularity and universality. Specifically at stake in it is circumcision, and Paul deliberately comes to Jerusalem accompanied by Titus, an uncircumcised follower. But in the background the question is: Who is called? What is it to be called? Is the call indexed by visible signs? And finally: Who is a subject? What marks a subject?

The Judeo-Christian faction, which maintains strict observance, asserts that the Christ-event does not abolish the old order. Its conception of the subject is dialectical. It is not a question of denying the power of the event. It is a question of asserting that its novelty conserves and sublates the traditional site of faith, that it incorporates it by exceeding it. The Christ-event accomplishes the Law; it does not terminate it. Thus the marks inherited from tradition (circumcision, for example) are still necessary. One might even say that, taken up and elevated by the new announcement, the latter become transfigured and are all the more active for it.

Paul finds himself leading the second faction. In his eyes, the event renders prior markings obsolete, and the new universality bears no privileged relation to the Jewish community. Certainly, the components of the event, its location, everything it mobilizes, have this community as their site. Paul himself is entirely of Jewish culture and cites the Old Testament far more frequently than the putative words of the living Christ. But although the event depends on its site *in its being*, it must be independent of it *in its truth effects*. Thus, it is not that communitarian marking (circumcision, rites, the meticulous observance of the Law) is indefensible or erroneous. It is that the posteventual imperative of truth renders the latter *indifferent* (which is worse). It has no signification, whether positive or negative. Paul is not opposed to circumcision. His rigorous assertion is "Circumcision is nothing, and uncircumcision is nothing" (Cor. I.7.19). This assertion is obviously sacrilegious for Judeo-Christians. But note that it is not, for all that, a Gentile-Christian assertion, since uncircumcision acquires no particular value through it, so that it is in no way to be insisted upon.

The debate, philosophically reconstructed, bears upon three concepts: interruption (what does an event interrupt, what does it preserve?); fidelity (what is it to be faithful to an evental interruption?); and marking (are there visible marks or signs of fidelity?). The fundamental interrogation is crystallized at the intersection of these three concepts: Who is the subject of the truth procedure?

We know of the Jerusalem conference's existence and stakes only through Paul's own brief narrative, and through its staging in the Acts. That it ended in compromise, in a sort of delimitation of spheres of influence, is certain. The formula for that compromise is: there are apostles working in the Jewish environment, and others working in the Gentile environment. Peter is apostle of the Jews; Paul, apostle of the Gentiles, the *ethnē* (translated as "nations," and in fact designating all peoples other than the Jewish people).

Paul relates the episode in his epistle to the Galatians, 2.1.10:

Then after fourteen years I went up again to Jerusalem with Barnabas, taking Titus along with me. I went up by revelation; and laid before them (but privately, before those who were of reputation) the gospel that I preach among the Gentiles, lest somehow I should be running or had run in vain. But even Titus, who was with me, was not compelled to be circumcised, though he was a Greek. But because of false brethren secretly brought in, who slipped in to spy out our freedom which we have in Christ Jesus, that they might bring us into bondage—to them we did not yield submission even for a moment, that the truth of the gospel might be preserved for you. And from those who were most esteemed (what they were makes no difference to me; God shows no partiality)—those, I say, who were of repute added nothing to me. But on the contrary, when they saw that I had been entrusted with the gospel of the uncircumcised, just as Peter had been entrusted the gospel of the circumcised (for he who worked through Peter for the mission to the circumcised, worked through me also for the Gentiles), and when they perceived the grace that was given to me, James and Cephas and John, who were reputed to be pillars, gave to me and Barnabas the right hands of fellowship, that we should go to the Gentiles and they to the circumcised, only they would have us remember the poor, which very thing I was eager to do.

This is an entirely political text, from which we must retain at least three points:

1. Whatever the ponderous character of this discourse, we deduce that the struggle was a fierce one. The Judeo-Christians of strict observance (probably those who were behind the disturbances at Antioch) are denounced as "false brethren," and it is clearly a question of knowing whether one is going to give in to pressure. There was an intercession by the historical apostles, Peter (Cephas), James, and John, who, carrying out their symbolic governing role in a spirit of rational compromise, approved some kind of empirical duality in the militant function. Nevertheless, we notice that nothing in this conclusion provides a clear indication as to which side has been taken on the fundamental issues. That Paul concern himself

with the Gentiles is one thing that he impose on them neither rites nor marks is another, one which the conference apparently does not decide.

2. The key moment in the text is the one in which Paul declares that his opponents spied out the "freedom which we have in Christ Jesus, that they might bring us into bondage." For freedom puts into play the question of the law, a question that will be central in Paul's discourse. What, in the final analysis, is the relation between law and subject? Is every subject configured in the form of a legal subjection? The Jerusalem conference resolves nothing, but lets conflicting experiences develop.

3. Everything, including Paul's defensive tone (he is visibly pleading for the recognized right to pursue his action), shows that the compromise was unstable, which is not to say it was without historical influence. On the contrary, that influence is considerable. By allowing Paul's action to develop at the same time as that of Judeo-Christians of strict observance, the Jerusalem conference ultimately prevents Christianity from becoming a Jewish sect, another precarious scission (in the wake of many others). But in curbing the zeal of those Gentile-Christians hostile to Judaism, and perhaps that of Paul himself, it prevented Christianity from being merely a new illuminism, one just as precarious because devoid of all basis in historical Judaism. The Jerusalem conference is genuinely foundational, because it endows Christianity with a twofold principle of opening and historicity. It thereby holds tight to the thread of the event as initiation of a truth procedure. That the event is new should never let us forget that it is such only with respect to a determinate situation, wherein it mobilizes the elements of its site. Admittedly, the conference does not seem able to fix the content of this difficult match between eventality and immanence to a situation. But that it manages to coordinate the possibility of this match empirically is already a lot. If it is true that Peter [Pierre] was the architect of the Jerusalem compromise, he deserves his title of cornerstone [*pierre angulaire*] of the Church.

That the situation remained tense even after the conference is attested to by the famous "incident at Antioch," which Paul mentions just after his narrative of the conference and which seems to have occurred at the end of the same year. This incident is passed over in silence in the Acts, which supports the view that the latter is an official document, whose function is to provide an account of the first decades of Christianity that would be as uniform, organizational, and "Roman" as possible.

What was this incident about? Peter is in Antioch (a tour of inspection?), where Paul has returned. The issue concerns whether one can share ritual meals with non-Jews. Peter begins by doing so, but seeing disciples of James entering, leaves the table. Paul takes it very badly. There is no doubt that he sees in Peter's behavior a betrayal of the initial compromise and a hypocritical position. The text still bears the imprint of genuine fury:

> But when Peter came to Antioch, I opposed him face to face, because he stood condemned. For before certain men came from James, he ate with the Gentiles; but when they came he drew back and separated himself, fearing the circumcision party. And with him the rest of the Jews acted insincerely, so that even Barnabas was carried away by their insincerity. But when I saw that they were not straightforward about the truth of the gospel, I said to Peter before them all, "If you, though a Jew, live like a Gentile, and not like a Jew, how can you compel the Gentiles to live like Jews?" (Gal. 2.11.14)

Paul will immediately break with Barnabas, who has been led astray by Peter. Everything indicates that he refused any compromise when it came to fidelity to principles.

The apparent enigma is the following: Why does Paul say to Peter that he (Peter), who is a Jew, lives in the manner of Gentiles? The answer supposes an implicit reference to the Jerusalem agreements. With respect to these agreements, what Peter did is tantamount to duplicity. It shows a hypocritical disrespect for a convention. For someone who claims to follow the Law, it amounts to a grave failing. One might say that Paul reproaches Peter with acting in a manner that fails to correspond to the image Peter himself claims to give of what it is to be a Jew. He thereby deprives himself of the right to force the Gentiles to conform to this image and to practice foreign rites.

It is impossible to overestimate the importance of the incident at Antioch. That Peter could display such inconsistency with regard to his own principles, such disloyalty to a past compromise, instills in Paul the idea that what is required are new principles. The incident reveals to him that the Law, in its previous imperative, is not, is no longer, tenable, even for those who claim to follow it. This will nourish one of Paul's essential theses, which is that the Law has *become* a figure of death: Peter's situation, at the very heart of the meager Christian "apparatus," a precarious, hypocritical, "reprehensible," and basically moribund situation so far as the requirements of action are concerned, furnished him with concrete proof of this. For Paul, it is no longer possible to maintain an equal balance between the Law, which is a principle of death for the suddenly ascendant truth, and the evental declaration, which is its principle of life.

Now the leader of a faction, and having learned from these major, "summit" confrontations, Paul sets off on his travels once again (Macedonia, Greece). The Acts presents us with the Hollywood version of these travels. One episode, as famous as it is unlikely, is that of the great speech Paul is said to have given before the Athenian philosophers (Stoics and Epicureans) "in the midst of the Areopagus." Perhaps we may retain, at least in its spirit, the episode's sorry conclusion: hearing Paul speak of the resurrection of the dead, the Greek philosophers burst out laughing and leave. It is in fact likely that Paul's discourse met with little success in Athens. The evidence is that Paul founded no group there. We find ourselves here on the second of Paul's major fronts (the first being the conflict with the Judeo-Christians): the contempt in which he holds philosophical wisdom. Basically, what gets him into difficulty in Athens is his antiphilosophy. In Corinthians I, we find a clear, albeit indirect, appraisal of these expeditions into philosophical territory by an antiphilosopher:

When I came to you, brethren, I did not come proclaiming to you the testimony of God in lofty words or wisdom. For I decided to know nothing among you except Jesus Christ and him crucified. And I was with you in weakness, and in much fear and trembling; and my speech and my message were not in persuasive words of wisdom, but in demonstration of the Spirit and power, that your faith might not rest in the wisdom of men, but in the power of God. (Cor. I.2.1–5)

The problem lies in knowing how, armed only with the conviction that declares the Christ-event, one is to tackle the Greek intellectual milieu, whose essential category is that of wisdom (*sophia*), and whose instrument is that of rhetorical superiority (*huperokhē logou*).

Speaking of logos, we should note that Paul writes in Greek, the Greek commonly spoken in the Orient of those days, which is a sort of international language (a bit like English today). It is in no way a contrived or esoteric language, but the Greek of traders and writers. We must restore to Paul's words, whose translations have become worn by centuries of obscurantism (all this "faith"! "charity"! "Holy Spirit"! What an extravagant waste of energy!), their contemporary, everyday currency; forbid ourselves from seeing them as a Church dialect. When Paul speaks of the subtleties of Greek, one must remember not only that the language of the literate, of the philosophers, is frozen, almost dead already, but also that the debate cannot be carried on from outside, according to the laborious transit between idioms. Conflict occurs within the same living language.

Paul opposes a show of spirit (*pneuma*, breath) and power (*dunamis*) to the armed wisdom of rhetoric. The wisdom of men is opposed to the power of God. It is thus a question of intervening *ouk en sophiai logou*, "without the wisdom of language." This maxim envelops a radical antiphilosophy; it is not a proposition capable of being supported by a *philosophia*. The essence of all this is that a subjective upsurge cannot be given as the rhetorical construction of a personal adjustment to the laws of the universe or nature.

Paul's appraisal seems sincere. There was a failure before the "Greeks." The Jews raise the question of the Law; the Greeks, that of Wisdom, of philosophy. Such are the two historical referents for Paul's enterprise. One must find the path for a thought that avoids both these referents. In public circumstances, this attempt at a diagonal trajectory rarely meets with success, rallying only a few anonymous companions. So begins every truth.

We are now under Nero's reign, and Paul's wish—we mentioned it earlier—is to go to Spain, which at the time represents the edge of the world. At the moment of departure, a new militant question arises, that of the collection.

In all the groups affiliated with the Christian declaration, funds destined for the Jerusalem community are collected. What does this contribution signify? Here, we encounter once again the conflict between tendencies refereed by the Jerusalem conference's feeble compromise.

The Judeo-Christians see in this paying of tribute an acknowledgment of the primacy of the historical apostles (Peter and the others), as well as the sign that elects Jerusalem—obvious center, along with the Temple, of the Jewish community—as natural center of the Christian movement. The collection thereby affirms a continuity between Jewish communitarianism and Christian expansionism. Lastly, through the collection, external groups recognize that they amount to a diaspora.

Paul gives an interpretation of the collection that is the exact opposite. By accepting their donations, the center ratifies the legitimacy of the Gentile-Christian groups. It demonstrates that neither membership of the Jewish community, nor the marks of that membership, nor being situated on the land of Israel are pertinent criteria for deciding whether a constituted group does or does not belong within the Christian sphere of influence.

Because he wishes to keep a watch on the collection's future development, as well as the meaning ascribed to it, Paul decides to accompany the funds to Jerusalem rather than go to Spain.

What happens next can only be conjectured. The most plausible account is the following. In Jerusalem, Paul is, in a sense, in the lion's den. He is required to conform to certain Jewish rites. Paul accepts, because, as he has written, he knows how to be "a Jew among Jews," just as he knows how to be a Greek among Greeks: subjective truth is indifferent to customs. He goes to the Temple. Subsequently, he becomes the target of an angry mob, because he has been accused of having smuggled a Gentile into the Temple. In the eyes of the Jewish religious administration, seconded on this point by the Roman occupier, who is in the habit of maintaining local customs, such an action is worthy of the death penalty.

Did Paul really commit the crime of which he is accused? The majority of historians think not. The truth is, no one knows. Paul is an activist, and nothing rules out the possibility that he believed such a provocation to be both possible and useful. In any case, he is arrested by a detachment of Roman soldiers at the moment when he is about to be lynched. It is the Romans who will initiate proceedings against him. Paul is taken to the garrison at Caesarea. Around 59, he appears before the governor, Festus (this much is certain). Since the accusation can lead to the death penalty, he claims his rights as a Roman citizen: a citizen charged with a capital offense has the right to be judged in Rome. Thus, he is transferred there, and it seems he remained prisoner there from 60 to 62. A brief allusion by Clement, around 90, leads one to think he was finally executed—whether following a formal trial, or during a persecution, no one can know.

None of Paul's texts refer to these episodes, and for good reason: all the authentic texts that have been handed down to us were certainly written prior to his arrest, which is to say that, so far as the final years of Paul's life are concerned, we remain, in reality, utterly ignorant. The voyage to Rome is recounted with a great wealth of detail in the Acts, following the familiar conventions of the seafaring adventure yarn. It is impossible to distinguish between the true and the false. The Acts ends strangely, not, as one might expect, with Paul's martyrdom, but with the edifying spectacle of an apostle continuing his proselytizing activity in Rome in perfect tranquility, which, along with many other details, testifies to the pro-Roman benevolence harbored by the author of the Acts.

Yet after all, Paul himself teaches us that it is not the signs of power that count, nor exemplary lives, but what a conviction is capable of, here, now, and forever.

3

Texts and Contexts

Paul's texts are letters, written by a leader to the groups he has started or backed. They cover a very brief period (from 50 to 58). They are militant documents sent to small groups of the converted. In no way are they narratives, in the manner of the Gospels, or theoretical treatises, of the kind later written by the Church Fathers, or lyrical prophecies, such as the Apocalypse attributed to John. They are *interventions*. From this point of view, they are more akin to the texts of Lenin than to Marx's *Capital*, or to the majority of texts by Lacan than to Freud's *Interpretation of Dreams*, or to Wittgenstein's lectures than to Russell's *Principia Mathematica*. This format, in which the opportunity for action takes precedent over the preoccupation with making a name for oneself through publications ("poubellications,"* as Lacan used to say), evinces one of the antiphilosopher's characteristic traits: he writes neither system nor treatise, nor even really a book. He propounds a speech of rupture, and writing ensues when necessary.

The enigma lies mainly in knowing how these topical texts were bequeathed to us, and what was responsible for their solemn and suspicious inclusion within that untouchable corpus known as the New Testament.

The canonical collection of "Paul's epistles" is late. It probably dates

*Portmanteau word combining *poubelles*, "trash cans," and *publications*, "publications."—Trans.

from the end of the second century. The oldest copies we possess come from the beginning of the third century and consist only of fragments. Moreover, as we indicated earlier, out of the thirteen letters contained in the New Testament at least six are certainly apocryphal, even if it seems probable that some of these originated from within Paul's "entourage."

Why and how did this corpus come to be canonized? Remember that Paul has no obvious historical legitimacy. He is not one of the twelve apostles. He knew nothing of the Lord's life. He caused many problems for the historical center in Jerusalem.

Four important remarks may illuminate this oddity.

1. Contrary to the persistent illusion harbored by the New Testament's canonical, multisecular order, and imposed on our spontaneous opinion, we will never tire of repeating that *Paul's epistles predate, by a long way, the composition of the Gospels.* Better still: Paul's epistles are, quite simply, *the oldest Christian texts to be handed down to us.* Of course, oral accounts of Christ's life, of his miracles, of his death, must have been abundantly propagated at the time of Paul's preaching. But no document establishing the details of that history has come down to us written prior to the year 70, which is to say, about ten years after Paul's death. If one dates the first epistle to the Thessalonians from 50, which is plausible, a twenty-year gap separates it from the writing of the first gospel (Mark's). Consequently, Paul enjoys a palpable anteriority so far as the written propagation of the Christian doctrine is concerned. And because his letters were copied and circulated very early on, it would probably have been difficult to simply ignore them when the time came (much later, at the end of the third century) to collect the new religion's founding documents.

2. With the partial exception of John's (which was written last, possibly around 90), the Gospels provide a genuine contrast to Paul's epistles, one to which we shall have occasion to return. Their aim is obviously to emphasize Jesus' *exploits*, his life's exceptional singularity. All the trusted staples of religious thaumaturgy and charlatanism are abundantly mobilized: miraculous cures, walking on water, divinations and announcements, resuscitation of the dead, abnormal meteorological phenomena, laying on of hands, instantaneous multiplication of victuals . . . Jesus' style, as recounted to us by the Gospels, is in complete accordance

with this itinerant magician's paraphernalia. Certainly, the choiceness of its aphorisms, and its shaping of the will to rupture, render it brilliant. Yet for all that, it is no less marked by the conventions of the genre: parables with a double meaning, obscure metaphors, apocalyptic imagery, carefully constructed undecidability as to the character's identity (Prophet? Messiah? Messenger of God? Son of God? New God descended on earth?).

Paul's texts retain almost nothing of all this, in spite of the fact that it must have been recounted in abundant detail among Christians of the first generation. It has often been noted that the empirical life of Jesus practically goes unmentioned in the epistles, as do all of the master's famous parables. Jesus' teachings, like his miracles, are splendidly ignored. Everything is brought back to a single point: Jesus, son of God (we shall see what this means), and Christ in virtue of this, died on the cross and was resurrected. The rest, all the rest, is of no real importance. Let us go further: the rest (what Jesus said and did) *is not what is real in conviction, but obstructs, or even falsifies it.* Only a concentrated style, shorn of the mannerisms of prophetic and thaumaturgical literature, can be appropriate to such a reduction. There is no doubt that Paul is a superlative writer: condensed, lapidary, knowing just when to unleash unusual and powerful images. Certain passages, as the poet Henry Bachau pointed out to us, combining a kind of violent abstraction with ruptures in tone designed to put pressure on the reader, to deprive him of all respite, resemble Shakespearean declamations. But ultimately, what matters so far as this prose is concerned is argumentation and delimitation, the forceful extraction of an essential core of thought. Consequently, there will be no parables, no learned obscurities, no subjective indecision, no veiling of truth. The paradox of faith must be brought out as it is, borne by prose into the light of its radical novelty.

The result of all this is that Paul's epistles are the only truly *doctrinal* texts in the New Testament. One understands why, for example, Luther considered that Paul's epistles, and they alone, contained the meaning of the Revelation, and he did not hide his low opinion of the synoptic Gospels, especially Luke's.

Without Paul's texts, the Christian message would remain ambiguous, with little to distinguish it from the overabundant prophetic and apocalyptic literature of the time. This is an important reason for their inclusion within the canonical corpus.

3. What happened between the writing of Paul's texts and that of the Gospels? A crucial event: the Jewish uprising against the Roman occupier, erupting in 66 (very probably after Paul's death), and culminating with Titus's destruction of the temple of Jerusalem in 70. This marks the true beginning of Jewish diaspora. Above all, it marks the end of Jerusalem's "central" significance for the Christian movement. Henceforth begins the process that will, little by little, turn Rome into the true capital of Christianity and historically erase that Jewish and Oriental origin of which Jerusalem, where the historic apostles resided, was the symbol.

Now, in several regards, it is Paul who, by virtue of his universal and de-centered vision of the construction of Christian enclaves, can be considered the genuine precursor for this displacement. There is no doubt that, for him, the structure of the Roman Empire, which means the world between the Orient and Spain, is more important than the preeminence of Jerusalem. That the most developed, most carefully crafted, most decisive of all his texts, especially so far as the break with Jewish law is concerned, was an epistle to the Romans, is an instance of the kind of fortuitousness whose symbolic function is irrecusable. Another major reason for inscribing Paul within the official corpus.

4. It is common knowledge that an organization puts together the compendium of its canonical texts when the time has come for it to secure its orientation against dangerous deviations, or struggle against threatening divisions. In this regard, the first centuries of Christianity are particularly fraught. So far as the question preoccupying us here is concerned, it is essential to take into account the upsurge of a heresy that one could call ultra-Pauline, that of Marcion, at the beginning of the second century.

Marcion, providing the cue for the long succession of heresies of Manichean tendency, maintains that the break between Christianity and Judaism, between (what we call) the Old Testament and the New Testament, must be considered to be absolute in a precise sense: *it is not the same God who is in question in these two religions.* The Old Testament deals with the God who created the world, and that God, as a consideration of the world as it is clearly establishes, is a malevolent being. Above this creator God, there exists a genuinely good God whose character is that of a Father and not a creator. We can say that, for Marcion, it is necessary to distinguish the symbolic Father (revealed through Christianity alone) from the creator, or real, father. The God of Christianity (the symbolic Father) is not known in the same sense as the God of the Old Testament (the progenitor). The latter is directly apprehensible through the narrative of his dark and capricious misdeeds. The former, which the world provides no trace of, and who for that reason cannot be known directly, or known according to the style of narrative, is accessible only through the coming of his Son. The result is that the Christian News is, purely and simply, the true God's mediating revelation, the event of the Father, which, at the same time, denounces the deception of that creator God whom the Old Testament tells us about.

Marcion's treatise, which has not been handed down to us, was called *The Anti-theses*. A crucial point: in it he maintained that Paul was the only authentic apostle; the other so-called apostles, with Peter at their head, remained under the auspice of the dark creator God. There were certainly good reasons why the heretic could enlist the "apostle of nations" in this way: chief among them Paul's struggle against the strictly observant Judeo-Christians, his evental conception of Christianity, and his polemic about the deathly aspect of the law. By pushing a little, one could arrive at Marcion's conception: the new gospel is an absolute beginning.

Nevertheless, there is no question but that this was an instance of manipulation. There is no text of Paul's from which one could draw anything resembling Marcion's doctrine. That the God whose son is Jesus Christ is the God spoken of in the Old Testament, the God of the Jews, is, for Paul, a ceaselessly reiterated and obvious fact. If there is a figure with whom Paul feels an affinity, and one whom he subtly uses to his own ends, it is that of Abraham. That Paul emphasizes rupture rather than continuity with Judaism is not in doubt. But this is a militant, and not an ontological, thesis. Divine unicity [*unicité*] bridges the two situations separated by the Christ-event, and at no moment is it cast into doubt.

In order to combat Marcion's dangerous heresy (which, in fact, abruptly backtracked on the Jerusalem compromise and threatened to turn Christianity into a sect devoid of all historical depth) the Church Fathers must have set out a reasonable and "centrist" version of Paul in opposition to ultra-Paulinism. The construction of the official Paul probably dates from here, a construction that is not devoid of various doctorings and deviations. The truth is that we know Marcion only through his orthodox opponents, either Irenaeus or Jerome. And correspondingly, Paul came to be known through this image of Paul that it was necessary to construct in opposition to those who, in accordance with an extremist vision of the Christian rupture, appropriated the founder's most radical statements. Herein lies a partial explanation for the inclusion of Paul's epistles within the final corpus: better for the Church, which was in the process of consolidating itself, to have a reasonable Paul on its side, than to have a Paul entirely turned over to the side of heresy. Nevertheless, this does not exclude the possibility that, on behalf of the cause, and by doctoring the genuine texts and fabricating false ones, the apostle came to be more or less "rectified," or his radicalism tempered, at the very least. An operation in which, as we saw earlier, the author of the Acts was already engaged at the end of the first century.

But in spite of everything, when one reads Paul, one is stupefied by the paucity of traces left in his prose by the era, genres, and circumstances. There is in this prose, under the imperative of the event, something solid and timeless, something that, precisely because it is a question of orienting a thought toward the universal *in its suddenly emerging singularity*, but independently of all anecdote, is intelligible to us without having to resort to cumbersome historical mediations (which is far from being the case for many passages in the Gospels, let alone for the opaque Apocalypse).

No one has better illuminated the uninterrupted contemporaneousness of Paul's prose than one of the greatest poets of our time, Pier Paolo Pasolini, who, it must be said, with his two first names was at the heart of the problem, through the signifier alone.

Pasolini, for whom the question of Christianity intersected with that of communism, or alternatively, the question of saintliness intersected with that of the militant, wanted to make a film about Saint Paul transplanted into the contemporary world. The film was never made, but we possess a detailed script for it, one that was translated into French and published by Flammarion.

Pasolini's aim was to turn Paul into a contemporary without modifying any of his statements. He wanted to restore, in the most direct, most violent way, the conviction of Paul's intrinsic actuality. It was a question of explicitly telling the spectator that it was possible to imagine Paul among us, here, today, in his full physical existence. That it is our society Paul is addressing, that it is for us he weeps, threatens and forgives, attacks and tenderly embraces. He wanted to say: Paul is our fictional contemporary because the universal content of his preaching, obstacles and failures included, remains absolutely real.

For Pasolini, Paul, in revolutionary fashion, wanted to destroy a model of society based on social inequality, imperialism, and slavery. There resides in him the holy will to destruction. Certainly, in the film as envisioned, Paul fails, and this failure is even more internal than public. But he pronounces the truth of the world, and does so in the same unaltered terms in which he spoke almost two thousand years ago.

Pasolini's thesis is threefold:

1. Paul is our contemporary because the sudden eruption of chance, the event, the pure encounter, are always at the origin of a saintliness. Moreover, today, the figure of the saint is necessary, even if the contents of the initiating encounter may vary.

2. By transplanting Paul, along with all his statements, into our century, one sees them encountering there a real society every bit as criminal and corrupt, but infinitely more supple and resistant, than that of the Roman Empire.

3. Paul's statements are endowed with a timeless legitimacy.

The central theme is situated in the relation between actuality and saintliness. Whenever the world of History tends to escape into mystery, abstraction, pure interrogation, it is the world of the divine (of saintliness) which, eventually [*événementiellement*] descended among humans, becomes concrete, operative.

The film script charts the trajectory of a saintliness within an actuality. How is the transposition effected?

Rome is New York, capital of American imperialism. Jerusalem, cultural seat occupied by the Romans, seat also of intellectual conformity, is Paris under the German heel. The small, nascent Christian community is represented by the Resistance, while the Pharisees are the Pétainists.

Paul is French, from a comfortable bourgeois background, a collaborator, hunting members of the Resistance.

Damascus is the Barcelona of Franco's Spain. The fascist Paul goes on a mission to see supporters of Franco. On the road to Barcelona, traveling through southwestern France, he has an illumination. He joins the camp of the antifascist Resistance.

We then follow him as he travels around preaching resistance, in Italy, in Spain, in Germany. Athens, the Athens of the sophists who refused to listen to Paul, is represented by contemporary Rome, by those petty Italian intellectuals and critics whom Pasolini detested. Finally, Paul goes to New York, where he is betrayed, arrested, and executed in sordid circumstances.

The principal aspect in this trajectory gradually becomes that of betrayal, its wellspring being that what Paul creates (the Church, the Organization, the Party) turns against his own inner saintliness. Here, Pasolini finds support in a major tradition (one we shall examine later) that sees in Paul not so much a theoretician of the Christian event as the tireless creator of the Church. A man of the institution: in short, a militant of the Third International. For Pasolini, reflecting on communism through Paul, the Party is what, little by little, inverts saintliness into priesthood through the narrow requirements of militantism. How does genuine saintliness (which Pasolini unhesitatingly recognizes in Paul) bear the ordeal of a History that is at once fleeting and monumental, one in which it constitutes an exception rather than an operation? It can only do so by hardening itself, by becoming authoritarian and organized. But that hardness, which is supposed to preserve it from all corruption by History, reveals itself to be an essential corruption, that of the saint by the priest. It is the almost necessary movement of an internal betrayal. And this internal betrayal is captured by an external betrayal, so that Paul will be denounced. The traitor is Saint Luke, portrayed as an agent of the Devil, writing the Acts of the Apostles in an unctuous and emphatic style with the aim of eradicating saintliness. Such is Pasolini's interpretation of the

Acts: it is a question of writing Paul's life as if all he had ever been was a priest. The Acts, and more generally, the official image of Paul, present us with the saint erased by the priest. This is a falsification, because Paul *is* a saint. But the film script allows us to understand the truth behind this deception: in Paul, the immanent dialectic of saintliness and actuality constructs a subjective figure of the priest. Paul also dies to the extent that saintliness has darkened within him.

A saintliness immersed in an actuality such as that of the Roman Empire, or equally, that of contemporary capitalism, can protect itself only by creating, with all requisite severity, a Church. But this Church turns saintliness into priesthood.

The most surprising thing in all this is the way in which Paul's texts are transplanted unaltered, and with an almost unfathomable natural-ness, into the situations in which Pasolini deploys them: war, fascism, American capitalism, the petty debates of the Italian intelligentsia . . . The universal value of the core of Paul's thought, as well as of the time-lessness of his prose, successfully undergoes this artistic trial, and Paul emerges strangely victorious.

4

Theory of Discourses

When Paul is designated by the Jerusalem conference as apostle of the *ethnē* (rather inaccurately translated as "nations"), one might think that, henceforth, his preaching is to relate to an absolutely open multiple of peoples and customs, in fact, to all the human subsets of the empire, which are extremely numerous. Yet consistently, Paul only explicitly mentions two entities—the Jews and the Greeks—as if this metonymic representation sufficed, or as if, with these two referents, the multiple of the *ethnē* had been exhausted so far as the Christian revelation and its universal destination is concerned. What is the status of this Jew/Greek couple, which single-handedly stands in for the empire's "national" complexity?

One basic reply consists in saying that "Greek" is equivalent to "Gentile," and that ultimately the multiplicity of nations is covered by the straightforward opposition between Jewish monotheism and official polytheism. However, this reply is unconvincing, because when Paul talks about the Greeks, or about Greek, he only very rarely associates these words with a religious belief. As a rule, he is talking about wisdom, and hence about philosophy.

It is essential to understand that in Paul's lexicon, "Jew" and "Greek" do not designate anything we might spontaneously understand by means of the word "nation," which is to say an objective human set grasped in terms of its beliefs, customs, language, territory, and so forth. Neither is it constituted, legalized religions that are being referred to. In reality, "Jew" and "Greek" *are subjective dispositions*. More precisely, they refer to what Paul considers to be the two coherent intellectual figures of the world he inhabits, or what could be called *regimes of discourse*. When theorizing about the Jew and the Greek, Paul is in fact presenting us with a schema of discourses. And this schema is designed to position a third discourse, his own, in such a way as to render its complete originality apparent. Like Lacan, who considers analytical discourse only in order to inscribe it within a mobile schema wherein it is connected to the discourses of the master, the hysteric, and the university, Paul institutes "Christian discourse" only by distinguishing its operations from those of Jewish discourse and Greek discourse. And the analogy is all the more striking in that, as we shall see, Paul accomplishes his objective only by defining a fourth discourse, which could be called mystical, as the margin for his own. As if every schema of discourses had to configure a quadrangle. But is it not Hegel who illuminates this point when, at the end of his *Logic*, he shows that the absolute Knowledge of a ternary dialectic requires a fourth term?

What is Jewish discourse? The subjective figure constituted by it is that of the prophet. But a prophet is one who abides in the requisition of signs, one who signals, testifying to transcendence by exposing the obscure to its deciphering. Thus, Jewish discourse will be held to be, above all, the discourse of the sign.

What then is Greek discourse? The subjective figure constituted by it is that of the wise man. But wisdom consists in appropriating the fixed order of the world, in the matching of the logos to being. Greek discourse is *cosmic*, deploying the subject within the reason of a natural totality. Greek discourse is essentially the discourse of totality, insofar as it upholds the *sophia* (wisdom as internal state) of a knowledge of *phusis* (nature as ordered and accomplished deployment of being).

Jewish discourse is a discourse of exception, because the prophetic sign, the miracle, election, designate transcendence as that which lies beyond the natural totality. The Jewish nation itself is at once sign, miracle, and election. It is constitutively exceptional. Greek discourse bases itself on the cosmic order so as to adjust itself to it, while Jewish discourse bases itself on the exception to this order so as to turn divine transcendence into a sign.

Paul's profound idea is that Jewish discourse and Greek discourse are the two aspects of the same figure of mastery. For the miraculous exception of the sign is only the "minus-one," the point of incoherence, which the cosmic totality requires in order to sustain itself. In the eyes of Paul the Jew, the weakness of Jewish discourse is that its logic of the exceptional sign is only valid *for* the Greek cosmic totality. The Jew is in exception to the Greek. The result is, firstly, that neither of the two discourses can be universal, because each supposes the persistence of the other; and secondly, that the two discourses share the presupposition that the key to salvation is given to us within the universe, whether it be through direct mastery of the totality (Greek wisdom), or through mastery of a literal tradition and the deciphering of signs (Jewish ritualism and prophetism). For Paul, whether the cosmic totality be envisaged as such or whether it be deciphered on the basis of the sign's exception, institutes in every case a theory of salvation tied to mastery (to a law), along with the grave additional inconvenience that the mastery of the wise man and that of the prophet, necessarily unaware of their identity, divide humanity in two (the Jew *and* the Greek), thereby blocking the universality of the Announcement.

Paul's project is to show that a universal logic of salvation cannot be reconciled with any law, be it one that ties thought to the cosmos, or one that fixes the effects of an exceptional election. It is impossible that the starting point be the Whole, but just as impossible that it be an exception to the Whole. Neither totality nor the sign will do. One must proceed from the event as such, which is a-cosmic and illegal, refusing integration into any totality and signaling nothing. But proceeding from the event delivers no law, no form of mastery, be it that of the wise man or the prophet.

One may also say: Greek and Jewish discourse are both discourses *of the Father*. That is why they bind communities in a form of obedience (to the Cosmos, the Empire, God, or the Law). Only that which will present itself *as a discourse of the Son* has the potential to be universal, detached from every particularism.

This figure of the son evidently fascinated Freud, just as it underlies Pasolini's identification with the apostle Paul. In the case of the former, with regard to that Jewish monotheism for which Moses is the decentered founding figure (the Egyptian as Other of the origin), Christianity raises the question of the relation that sons have to the Law, with the symbolic murder of the Father in the background. In the case of the latter, the power of thought intrinsic to homosexual desire is turned toward the advent of an egalitarian humanity, wherein the concordance of the sons cancels, to the benefit of the love of the mother, the crushing symbolism of the fathers, which is embodied in institutions (the Church, or the Communist Party). In addition, Pasolini's Paul is as though torn between the saintliness of the son—linked, given the law of the world, to abjection and death—and the ideal of power proper to the father, which drives him to create a coercive apparatus in order to dominate History.

For Paul, the emergence of the instance of the son is essentially tied to the conviction that "Christian discourse" is absolutely *new*. The formula according to which God sent us his Son signifies primarily an intervention within History, one through which it is, as Nietzsche will put it, "broken in two," rather than governed by a transcendent reckoning in conformity with the laws of an epoch. The sending (birth) of the son names this rupture. That it is the son, not the father, who is exemplary, enjoins us not to put our trust any longer in any discourse laying claim to the form of mastery.

That discourse has to be that of the son means that one must be neither Judeo-Christian (prophetic mastery), nor Greco-Christian (philosophical mastery), nor even a synthesis of the two. The opposing of a diagonalization of discourses to their synthesis is a constant preoccupation of Paul's. It is John who, by turning the logos into a principle, will synthetically inscribe Christianity within the space of the Greek logos, thereby subordinating it to anti-Judaism. This is certainly not the way Paul proceeds. For him, Christian discourse can maintain fidelity to the son only by delineating a third figure, equidistant from Jewish prophecy and the Greek logos.

This attempt can only be accomplished through a sort of decline of the figure of the Master. And since there are two figures of the master, the one that legitimates itself on the basis of the cosmos, the master in wisdom, the Greek master, and the one that legitimates itself according to the power of exception, the master of the letter and of signs, the Jewish master, Paul will be neither a prophet nor a philosopher. Accordingly, the triangulation he proposes is: prophet, philosopher, apostle.

What exactly does "apostle" (*apostolos*) mean? Nothing empirical or historical in any case. In order to be an apostle, it is not necessary to have been a companion of Christ, a witness to the event. Paul, who claims his legitimacy only from himself, and who, according to his own expression, has been "called to be an apostle," explicitly challenges the pretension of those who, in the name of what they were and saw, believe themselves to be guarantors of truth. He calls them "those who are most esteemed," and seems, for his own part, not to share this esteem. He also adds, "What they were makes no difference to me; God shows no partiality" (Gal. 2.6). An apostle is neither a material witness, nor a memory.

At a time when the importance of "memory" as the guardian of meaning and of historical consciousness as a substitute for politics is being urged on us from all sides, the strength of Paul's position cannot fail to escape us. For it is certainly true that memory does not prevent anyone from prescribing time, including the past, according to its present determination. I do not doubt the necessity of remembering the extermination of the Jews, or the action of Resistance fighters. But I note that the neo-Nazi maniac harbors a collector's memory for the period he reveres, and that, remembering Nazi atrocities in minute detail, he relishes and wishes he could repeat them. I see a number of informed people, some of them historians, conclude on the basis of their memory of the Occupation and the documents they have accumulated, that Pétain had many virtues. Whence the obvious conclusion that "memory" cannot settle any issue. There invariably comes a moment when what matters is to declare in one's own name that what took place took place, and to do so because what one envisages with regard to the *actual* possibilities of a situation requires it. This is certainly Paul's conviction: the debate about the Resurrection is no more a debate between historians and witnesses in his eyes than that about the existence of the gas chambers is in mine. We will not ask for proofs and counterproofs. We will not enter into debate with erudite anti-Semites, Nazis under the skin, with their superabundance of "proofs" that no Jew was ever mistreated by Hitler.

To which it is necessary to add that the Resurrection—which is the point at which our comparison obviously collapses—is not, in Paul's own eyes, of the order of fact, falsifiable or demonstrable. It is pure event, opening of an epoch, transformation of the relations between the possible and the impossible. For the interest of Christ's resurrection does not lie in itself, as it would in the case of a particular, or miraculous, fact. Its genuine meaning is that it testifies to the possible victory over death, a death that Paul envisages, as we shall see later in detail, not in terms of facticity, but in terms of subjective disposition. Whence the necessity of constantly linking resurrection to *our* resurrection, of proceeding from singularity to universality and vice versa: "If the dead do not resurrect, Christ is not resurrected either. And if Christ is not resurrected, your faith is in vain" (Cor. I.15.16). In contrast to the fact, the event is measurable only in accordance with the universal multiplicity whose possibility it prescribes. It is in this sense that it is grace, and not history.

The apostle is then he who names this possibility (the Gospels, the Good News, comes down to this: we *can* vanquish death). His discourse is one of pure fidelity to the possibility opened by the event. It cannot, therefore, in any way (and this is the upshot of Paul's antiphilosophy) fall under the remit of knowledge. The philosopher knows eternal truths; the prophet knows the univocal sense of what will come (even if he delivers it only through figures, through signs). The apostle, who declares an unheard-of possibility, one dependent on an evental grace, properly speaking knows nothing. To imagine that one knows, when it is a question of subjective possibilities, is fraudulent: "He who thinks he knows something [*egnōkenai ti*], does not yet know as he ought to know" (Cor. I.8.2). How is one to know when one is an apostle? According to the truth of a declaration and its consequences, which, being without proof or visibility, emerges at that point where knowledge, be it empirical or conceptual, breaks down. In characterizing Christian discourse from the point of salvation, Paul does not hesitate to say: "Knowledge [*gnōsis*] will disappear"(Cor. I.13.8).

The text wherein the characteristics of Christian discourse, insofar as it delineates the subjective figure of the apostle, are recapitulated under the sign of an evental disappearance of the virtues of knowledge, can be found in the first epistle to the Corinthians:

For Christ did not send me to baptize but to preach the gospel, and not with elo-quent wisdom, lest the cross of Christ be emptied of its power. For the preach-ing of the cross is folly to those who are perishing, but to us who are saved it is the power of God. For it is written, "I will destroy the wisdom of the wise, and thwart the cleverness of the clever." Where is the wise man? Where is the scribe? Where is the debater of this age? Has not God made foolish the wisdom of the world? For since, in the wisdom of God, the world did not know God through wisdom, it pleased God through the folly of what we preach to save those who believe. For Jews demand signs and Greeks seek wisdom, but we preach Christ crucified, a stumbling block to Jews and a folly to Gentiles, but to those who are called, both Jews and Greeks, Christ the power of God, and the wisdom of God. For the foolishness of God is wiser than men, and the weakness of God is stronger than men.

For consider your call, brethren; not many of you were wise according to worldly standards, not many were powerful, not many were of noble birth, but God chose the foolish things of the world to confound the wise, and God chose the weak things of the world to confound the strong; God chose what is base and despised in the world, and even things that are not, to bring to nought things that are, so that no one might glorify himself in his presence. (Cor. I.1.17–29)

The announcement of the gospel is made without the wisdom of language "lest the cross of Christ be emptied of its power." What does it mean for the event whose sign is the cross to be emptied of its power? Simply, that this event is of such a character as to render the philosophi-cal logos incapable of declaring it. The underlying thesis is that one of the phenomena by which one recognizes an event is that the former is like a point of the real [*point de réel*] *that puts language into deadlock.* This dead-lock is folly (*mōria*) for Greek discourse, which is a discourse of reason, and it is a scandal (*skandalon*) for Jewish discourse, which insists on a sign of divine power and sees in Christ nothing but weakness, abjection, and contemptible peripeteia. What imposes the invention of a new discourse, and of a subjectivity that is neither philosophical nor prophetic (the apos-tle), is precisely that it is only by means of such invention that the event finds a welcome and an existence in language. For established languages, it is inadmissible because it is genuinely unnamable.

From a more ontological viewpoint, it is necessary to maintain that Christian discourse legitimates neither the God of wisdom (because God has chosen the foolish things), nor the God of power (because God has chosen the weak and base things). But what unites these two traditional determinations, and provides the basis for their rejection, is deeper still. Wisdom and power are attributes of God to the extent that they are attributes of being. God is said to be the sovereign intellect, or to govern the world and men's destiny to the precise extent that pure intellect is the supreme point of being specified by a wisdom, and universal power that whose innumerable signs—equally signs of Being as that which is beyond beings—can be distributed or applied to the becoming of men. One must, in Paul's logic, go so far as to say that *the Christ-event testifies that God is not the god of Being, is not Being.* Paul prescribes an anticipatory critique of what Heidegger calls onto-theology, wherein God is thought as supreme being, and hence as the measure for what being as such is capable of.

The most radical statement in the text we are commenting on is in effect the following: "God has chosen the things that are not [*ta mē onta*] in order to bring to nought those that are [*ta onta*]." That the Christ-event causes nonbeings rather than beings to arise as attesting to God; that it consists in the abolition of what all previous discourses held as existing, or being, gives a measure of the ontological subversion to which Paul's antiphilosophy invites the declarant or militant.

It is through the invention of a language wherein folly, scandal, and weakness supplant knowing reason, order, and power, and wherein nonbeing is the only legitimizable affirmation of being, that Christian discourse is articulated. In Paul's eyes, this articulation is incompatible with any prospect (and there has been no shortage of them, almost from the time of his death onward) of a "Christian philosophy."

Paul's position on the newness of Christian discourse relative to all forms of knowledge and the incompatibility between Christianity and philosophy is so radical that it unsettles even Pascal. Yes, Pascal, that other great figure of antiphilosophy, he who, under the modern conditions of the subject of science, seeks to identify the Christian subject, he who condemns Descartes ("useless and uncertain"), he who explicitly opposes the God of Abraham, Isaac, and Jacob, to the God of the philosophers and scientists; Pascal does not manage to understand Paul.

Consider for example fragment 547 of the *Pensées*:

We know God only through Jesus Christ. Without this mediator, all communication with God is withdrawn; through Jesus Christ, we know God. All those who claimed to know God and sought to prove it without Jesus Christ furnished only impotent proofs. But in order to prove Jesus Christ, we have the prophecies, which are solid and palpable proofs. And these prophecies, having been accomplished, and proved true by the event, mark the certainty of those truths, and hence, the proof of Jesus Christ's divinity. By him and through him, we thus know God. Without that and without Scripture, without original sin, without the promise and advent of a necessary Mediator, one cannot furnish absolute proof of God, or teach either sound doctrine or sound morality. But by Jesus Christ and through Jesus Christ, one furnishes proof of God, and one teaches morality and doctrine. Thus, Jesus Christ is men's true God.

But at the same time, we recognize our misery, for this God is nothing but the Redressor of our misery. Thus, we may properly know God only by recognizing our iniquities. And those who have known God without knowing their misery have not glorified him but glorified themselves. *Quia . . . non cognovit per sapientiam . . . placuit Deo per stultitiam praedicationis salvos facere.*

This text easily allows us to identify what Pascal and Paul have in common: the conviction that the fundamental declaration has to do with Christ. But from that point on, things begin to diverge from a twofold point of view.

1. With Paul, we notice a complete absence of the theme of mediation. Christ is not a mediation; he is not that through which we *know* God. Jesus Christ is the pure event, and as such is not a function, even were it to be a function of knowledge, or revelation.

We are confronted here with a profound general problem: Can one conceive of the event as a function, as a mediation? We should mention in passing that this question ran through the entire epoch of revolutionary politics. For many of those faithful to it, the revolution is not what arrives, but what must arrive so that there can be something else; it is communism's mediation, the moment of the negative. Similarly, for Pascal, Christ is a mediating figure, ensuring that we do not remain in a state of abandonment and ignorance. For Paul, by contrast, just as for those who think a revolution is a self-sufficient sequence of political truth, Christ is *a coming* [*une venue*]; he is what interrupts the previous regime of discourses. Christ is, in himself and for himself, *what happens to us*. And what is it that happens to us thus? We are relieved of the law. But the idea of mediation remains legal; it enters into composition with wisdom, with philosophy. This question is decisive for Paul, because it is only by being relieved of the law that one truly becomes a son. And an event is falsified if it does not give rise to a universal becoming-son. Through the event, we enter into filial equality. For Paul, one is either a slave, or a son. He would certainly have considered the Pascalian idea of mediation as still bound to the legality of the Father, and hence as a muted negation of evental radicality.

2. Only reluctantly does Pascal admit that Christian discourse is a discourse of weakness, folly, and nonbeing. Paul says "folly of our preaching"; Pascal translates it as "knowledge of our own ignorance." This is not a Pauline theme; misery for Paul always consisting in a subjection to law. Pascalian antiphilosophy is classical in that it remains bound to the conditions for knowledge. For Paul, it is not a question of knowledge, but of the advent of a subject. Can there be another subject, a subjective path other than the one we know, and which Paul calls the subjective path of the flesh? This is the one and only question, which no protocol of knowledge can help settle.

Because of his desire to convince the modern libertine, Pascal is haunted by the question of knowledge. His strategy requires that one be able to reasonably *prove* the superiority of the Christian religion. It is necessary to establish that the event fulfills the prophecies—singularly so in the case of Christ's coming—that the New Testament legitimates the rational deciphering of the Old one (via the doctrine of manifest and hidden meaning). Correspondingly, the Old Testament draws its coherence from that which, within it, signals toward the New.

Paul would have seen in the Pascalian theory of the sign and of double meaning an unacceptable concession to Jewish discourse, just as he would have seen in the probabilistic argumentation of the wager, as well as in the dialectical ratiocinations about the two infinites, an unacceptable concession to philosophical discourse. For Paul, the event has not come to prove something; it is pure beginning. Christ's resurrection is neither an argument nor an accomplishment. There is no proof of the event; nor is the event a proof. Knowledge comes for Pascal where, for Paul, there is only faith. As a result, unlike Paul, Pascal considers it important to balance Christian "folly" with a classical apparatus of wisdom:

Our religion is wise and foolish. Wise, because it is the most knowledgeable, and the most well-based in miracles, prophecies, and so on. Foolish, because none of this makes one belong to it; it serves as a pretext for the condemnation of those who do not belong, but not for the belief of those who do belong. It is the cross that makes them believe, *ne evacuata sit crux*. And thus Saint Paul, who came in wisdom and signs, says he came neither in wisdom nor signs, because he came to convert. But those who come only to convince can say that they come in wisdom and signs.

We have here a perfect, entirely non-Pauline example of the Pascalian technique. Let us give it a name: balanced contradiction. Pascal opposes conversion and conviction. In order to convert, it is doubtless necessary to be on the side of folly, of the preaching of the cross. But in order to convince, it is necessary to install oneself in the element of proof (miracles, prophecies, and so on). For Pascal, Paul hides his true identity. He acts through signs and wisdom, but because he wishes to convert, he claims not to.

This Pascalian reconstruction of Paul is in fact indicative of Pascal's reticence in the face of Pauline radicalism. For Paul expressly rejects signs, which belong to the order of Jewish discourse, as well as wisdom, which belongs to Greek discourse. He presents himself as deploying a subjective figure that has been subtracted from both, which means that neither miracles, nor the rational exegesis of prophecies, nor the order of the world have any value when it comes to instituting the Christian subject. But for Pascal, miracles and prophecies are at the heart of the question: "It is not possible to reasonably believe against miracles" (frag. 815); "The greatest of Christ's proofs are prophecies" (frag. 706). Without prophecies or miracles, we would have no proof, and the superiority of Christianity could not be upheld before the tribunal of reason, which means that we would have no chance of convincing the modern libertine.

For Paul, on the contrary, it is precisely the absence of proof that constrains faith, which is constitutive of the Christian subject.

So far as the prophecies are concerned, whether the Christ-event is their realization is practically absent from Paul's preaching considered as a whole. Christ is precisely incalculable.

So far as miracles are concerned, Paul, subtle politician, does not risk denying their existence. One even finds him occasionally hinting that, like such and such among his rival thaumaturges, he is capable of performing them. He too could glory in supernatural raptures, if he so wished. But this is what he will not do, exhibiting instead the subject's weakness and the absence of signs and proofs, as supreme proof. The decisive passage is in Corinthians. II.12.1–11:

I must glory; there is nothing to be gained by it, but I will come to visions and revelations of the Lord. I know a man in Christ who fourteen years ago was caught up to the third heaven . . . and he heard things that cannot be told, which it is not lawful for man to utter. . . . Though if I wish to glorify myself, I shall not be a fool, for I shall be speaking the truth. But I refrain from it, so that no one may think more of me than he sees in me or hears from me. . . . The Lord said to me: "My grace is sufficient for you, for my strength is made perfect in weakness." I will all the more gladly glory in my weakness, that the power of Christ may rest upon me . . . for when I am weak, then I am strong.

Clearly then, for Paul, miracles exist and have concerned him. He delineates a particular subjective figure, that of the "exalted" man, who has perhaps been summoned out of his body during the course of his life. But this figure is precisely not the one the apostle is going to present. The apostle must be accountable only for what others see and hear, which is to say, his declaration. He has no need to glorify himself in the name of that other subject who has spoken with God, and who is like an Other within himself ("On behalf of such a man as this I will glory, but I will not glory on my own behalf, except in my weaknesses" [Cor. II.12.5]). Christian discourse must, unwaveringly, refuse to be the discourse of miracle, so as to be the discourse of the conviction that bears a weakness within itself.

Let us note in passing that Paul delineates, as if in shadowy outline, a fourth possible discourse, besides the Greek (wisdom), the Jew (signs), and the Christian (evental declaration). This discourse, which Pascal tries to bring into the light of classical reason, would be that of the miracle, and Paul gives it a name: subjective discourse of glorification. It is the discourse of the ineffable, the discourse of nondiscourse. It is the subject as silent and mystical intimacy, inhabited by "things that cannot be told [*arrhēta rhēmata*]," which would be better translated as "unutterable utterances" (*dires indiçibles*), only experienced by the subject who has been visited by miracle. But this fourth subjective figure, splitting the apostle again, must not enter into the declaration, which, on the contrary, nourishes itself on the inglorious evidence of weakness. It is kept off to one side, and unlike Pascal, Paul is convinced that Christian discourse has nothing to gain by using it to glorify itself. The fourth discourse (miraculous, or mystical) must remain *unaddressed*, which is to say that it cannot enter into the realm of preaching. Paul is thereby ultimately more rational than Pascal: it is vain to want to justify a declaratory stance through the apparel of miracle.

For Paul, the fourth discourse will remain a mute supplement, enclosing the Other's share in the subject. He refuses to let addressed discourse, which is that of the declaration of faith, justify itself through an unaddressed discourse, whose substance consists in unutterable utterances.

I believe this to be an important indication, one that concerns every militant of a truth. There is never occasion to try to legitimate a declaration through the private resource of a miraculous communication with truth. Let us leave truth to its subjective "voicelessness," for only the work of its declaration constitutes it.

I shall call "obscurantist" every discourse that presumes to legitimate itself on the basis of an unaddressed discourse. It has to be said that Pascal, when he wants to establish the preeminence of Christianity on the basis of miracles, is more obscurantist than Paul, probably because he wants to mask the pure event behind the (libertine's) fascination with a reckoning of chances.

Obviously, there is an element of cunning in Paul when he lets it be understood, without boasting about it, but without keeping silent about it either, that he is internally torn between the man of glorification, the "ravished" subject, and the man of declaration and weakness. But it cannot be denied that there is in him, and he is alone in this among the recognized apostles, an ethical dimension of antiobscurantism. For Paul will not permit the Christian declaration to justify itself through the ineffable. He will not allow the Christian subject to base his speech on the unutterable.

Paul is profoundly convinced that weakness will not be relieved through a hidden force. Power is fulfilled in weakness itself. Let us say that, for Paul, the ethics of discourse consists in never suturing the third discourse (the public declaration of the Christ-event) to the fourth (the glorification of the subject personally visited by miracle).

This ethics is profoundly coherent. Supposing I invoke (as Pascal does) the fourth discourse ("joys, tears of joy . . ."), and hence the private, unutterable utterances, in order to justify the third (that of Christian faith), *I relapse inevitably into the second discourse*, that of the sign, the Jewish discourse. For what is a prophecy if not a sign of what is to come? And what is a miracle if not a sign of the transcendence of the True? By granting to the fourth discourse (mysticism) no more than a marginal and inactive position, Paul keeps the radical novelty of the Christian declaration from relapsing into the logic of signs and proofs.

Paul firmly holds to the militant discourse of weakness. The declaration will have no other force than the one it declares and will not presume to convince through the apparel of prophetic reckoning, of the miraculous exception, or of the ineffable personal revelation. It is not the singularity of the subject that validates what the subject says; it is what he says that founds the singularity of the subject.

Pascal, by way of contrast, opts simultaneously for convincing exegesis, for the certainty of miracles, and for private meaning. He cannot relinquish proof, in the existential sense of the term, because he is of the classical era, and because his question is that of the Christian subject in the age of positive science.

Paul's antiphilosophy is nonclassical, because he accepts that there is no proof, even miraculous. Discourse's power of conviction is of another order, and it is capable of shattering the form of reasoning:

> For the weapons of our warfare are not carnal, but they have divine power to pull down strongholds. Through them, we destroy arguments and every proud obstacle to the knowledge of God and take every thought captive to obey Christ. (Cor. II.10.4–5)

It is with this regime of a discourse without proof, without miracles, without convincing signs, with this language of the naked event, which alone captures thought, that the magnificent and famous metaphor in Corinthians II.4.7 resonates: "But we have this treasure in earthen vessels, to show that the greatness of this power belongs to God and not to us."

The treasure is nothing but the event as such, which is to say a completely precarious having-taken-place. It must be borne humbly, with a precariousness appropriate to it. The third discourse must be accomplished in weakness, for therein lies its strength. It shall be neither logos, nor sign, nor ravishment by the unutterable. It shall have the rude harshness of public action, of naked declaration, without apparel other than that of its real content. There will be nothing but what each can see and hear. This is the earthen vessel.

Whoever is the subject of a truth (of love, of art, or science, or politics) knows that, in effect, he bears a treasure, that he is traversed by an infinite power. Whether or not this truth, so precarious, continues to deploy itself depends solely on his subjective weakness. Thus, one may justifiably say that he bears it only in an earthen vessel, day after day enduring the imperative—delicacy and subtle thought—to ensure that nothing shatters it. For with the vessel, and with the dissipation into smoke of the treasure it contains, it is he, the subject, the anonymous bearer, the herald, who is equally shattered.

5

The Division of the Subject

For Paul to maintain that, under the condition of the Christ-event, there has been a choice for things that are not against things that are, indicates in an exemplary way that in his eyes Christian discourse bears an absolutely new relation to its object. It is truly another figure of the real that is in question. This figure will deploy itself through the revelation that what constitutes the subject in its relation to this unheard-of real is not its unity, but its division. For, in reality, one subject is the weaving together of two subjective paths, which Paul names the flesh (*sarx*) and the spirit (*pneuma*). And the real in turn, insofar as it is in some way "grasped" by the two paths that constitute the subject, can be inflected according to two names: death (*thanatos*), or life (*zōē*). Insofar as the real is that which is thought in a subjectivating thought, it will be possible to maintain, according to a difficult, central aphorism, that to *gar phronēma tēs sarkos thanatos, to de phronēma tou pneumatos zōē* (Rom. 8.6), which, in spite of the difficulty of identifying death as a thought, one must not hesitate to translate as: "The thought of the flesh is death; the thought of the spirit is life."

After centuries during which this theme has been subjected to Platonizing (and therefore Greek) amendment, it has become almost impossible to grasp what is nevertheless a crucial point: *The opposition between spirit and flesh has nothing to do with the opposition between the soul and the body.* That is precisely why both the one and the other are thoughts, each identifying its real through an opposed name. If, evoking his existence as a persecutor prior to the Damascus conversion, Paul can affirm that "the very commandment which promised life, proved to be death to me" (Rom. 7.10), it is because a subjective maxim is always taken up in two possible senses, according to the flesh or according to the spirit, without it being possible for any substantial distinction of the Greek kind (soul and body, thought and sensibility) to unravel the subjective weaving. It is of the essence of the Christian subject to be divided, through its fidelity to the Christ-event, into two paths that affect every subject in thought.

The theory of subjective division disqualifies what other discourses identify as their object. It is, in the guise of the evental character of the real, the upsurge (*surrection*) of an *other* object.

In Greek discourse, the object is the finite cosmic totality as sojourn of thought. The real causes the (philosophical) desire to occupy the place allotted to you in adequate fashion, an allocation of places whose principle thought can recover. What thought identifies as properly real is a place, a sojourn, which the wise man knows it is necessary to consent to.

For Paul, the Christ-event, which shears and undoes the cosmic totality, is precisely what indicates the vanity of places. The real is attested to rather as the refuse from every place, there where the subject rehearses his weakness: "We have become, and are now, as the refuse of the world, the offscouring of all things" (Cor. I.4.13). One must therefore assume the subjectivity of refuse, and it is in the face of this abasement that the object of Christian discourse suddenly appears.

One will note the consonance with certain Lacanian themes concerning the ethics of the analyst: at the end of the treatment, the latter must, similarly, consent to occupy the position of refuse so that the analysand may endure some encounter with his or her real. By virtue of which, as Lacan notes, the analyst comes very close to saintliness.

For Jewish discourse, the object is elective belonging, exceptional alliance between God and his people. The entirety of the real is marked by the seal of that alliance and is gathered and manifested through the observance of the law. The real is set out on the basis of commandment.

The exception that constitutes it is conceivable only through the immemorial dimension of the law.

For Paul, the Christ-event is heterogeneous to the law, pure excess over every prescription, grace without concept or appropriate rite. The real can no more be what in elective exception becomes literalized in stone as timeless law (Jewish discourse), than it is what comes or returns to its place (Greek discourse). The "folly of our preaching" will exempt us from Greek wisdom by discontinuing the regime of places and totality. It will exempt us from the Jewish law by discontinuing observances and rites. The pure event can be reconciled neither with the natural Whole, nor with the imperative of the letter.

For him who considers that the real is pure event, Jewish and Greek discourses no longer present, as they continue to do in the work of Levinas, the paradigm of a major difference for thought. This is the driving force behind Paul's universalist conviction: that "ethnic" or cultural difference, of which the opposition between Greek and Jew is in his time, and in the empire as a whole, the prototype, is no longer significant with regard to the real, or to the new object that sets out a new discourse. No real distinguishes the first two discourses any longer, and their distinction collapses into rhetoric. As Paul declares, defying the evidence: "There is no distinction between Jew and Greek" (Rom. 10.12).

More generally, the moment the real is identified as event, making way for the division of the subject, the figures of distinction in discourse are terminated, because the position of the real instituted by them is revealed, through the retroaction of the event, to be illusory. Similarly, for the subject divided according to the paths through which the real is grasped—that of the flesh and that of the spirit—the "ethnic" subjects brought about by Jewish law just as by Greek wisdom become disqualified to the extent that they lay claim to the perpetuation of a full or undivided subject, whose particular predicates it would be possible to enumerate: genealogy, origin, territory, rituals, and so on.

To declare the nondifference between Jew and Greek establishes Christianity's potential universality; to found the subject as division, rather than as perpetuation of a tradition, renders the subjective element adequate to this universality by terminating the predicative particularity of cultural subjects.

There is no doubt that universalism, and hence the existence of any truth whatsoever, requires the destitution of established differences and the initiation of a subject divided in itself by the challenge of having nothing but the vanished event to face up to.

The whole challenge is that a discourse configuring the real as pure event be consistent. Is this possible? Paul tries to pursue this path.

Let us emphasize once more that, since the event that he takes to identify the real *is not* real (because the Resurrection is a fable), he is able to do so only by abolishing philosophy. This is probably what distinguishes Paul from contemporary antiphilosophers, who circumscribe the real-event within the realm of effective truths: "grand politics" for Nietzsche; the archi-scientific analytic act for Lacan; mystical aesthetics for Wittgenstein. The result is that, so far as philosophy is concerned, Paul's subjective position is far more abrupt than the therapeutic approach of the moderns, who all want to cure thought from the philosophical sickness. Paul's thesis is not that philosophy is an error, a necessary illusion, a phantasm, and so forth, but that there is no longer an admissible place for its pretension. The discourse of wisdom is definitively obsolete. This is what, manufactured though it probably is, is symbolized by the account in the Acts of the Apostles of Paul's encounter with the Greek philosophers on the Areopagus. It seems that the philosophers burst out laughing as soon as Paul's harangue touched on the only real of any import, which is the Resurrection. This Nietzschean laughter, in the sense of the Antichrist, expresses a disjunction, and not an opposition. The disjunctive formula is "the foolishness of God is wiser than men, and the weakness of God is stronger than men" (Cor. I.1.25). The primacy of foolishness over wisdom, and of weakness over strength, commands the dissipation of the formula of mastery, without which philosophy cannot exist. Henceforth, it is no longer even possible to discuss philosophy; one must declare its *effective* expiration, along with that of every figure of mastery.

Paul never stops telling us that the Jews are looking for signs and "demanding miracles," that the Greeks are "looking for wisdom" and asking questions, that the Christians declare Christ crucified. To demand—to question—to declare: such are the verbal forms proper to the three discourses, their subjective postures.

If one demands signs, he who performs them in abundance be-comes a master for him who demands them. If one questions philosoph-ically, he who can reply becomes a master for the perplexed subject. But he who declares without prophetic or miraculous guarantees, without ar-guments or proofs, does not enter into the logic of the master. Declara-tion, in effect, is not affected by the emptiness (of the demand) wherein the master installs himself. He who declares does not attest to any lack and remains withdrawn from its fulfillment by the figure of the master. This is why it is possible for him to occupy the place of the son. To de-clare an event is to become the son of that event. That Christ is Son is emblematic of the way in which the evental declaration filiates the de-clarant.

Philosophy knows only disciples. But a son-subject is the opposite of a disciple-subject, because he is one whose life is beginning. The pos-sibility of such a beginning requires that God the Father has filiated him-self, that he has assumed the form of the son. It is by consenting to the figure of the son, as expressed by the enigmatic term "sending," that the Father causes us ourselves to come forth universally as sons. The son is he for whom nothing is lacking, for he is nothing but beginning. "So through God you are no longer a slave but a son, and if a son then an heir" (Gal. 4.7).

The father, always particular, withdraws behind his son's universal evidence. It is quite true that all postevental universality equalizes sons through the dissipation of the particularity of the fathers. Whence the way in which every truth is marked by an indestructible *youthfulness.*

Later, theology will indulge in all sorts of contortions in order to es-tablish the substantial identity of Father and Son. Paul has no interest at all in such Trinitarian questions. The antiphilosophical metaphor of the "sending of the son" is enough for him, for he requires only the event and refuses all philosophical reinscription of this pure occurrence by means of the philosophical vocabulary of substance and identity.

The resurrected Son filiates all of humanity. This constitutes the uselessness of the figure of knowledge and its transmission. For Paul, the figure of knowledge is itself a figure of slavery, like that of the law. The figure of mastery is in reality a fraud. One must depose the master and found the equality of sons.

The most powerful expression of this equality, necessary correlate of this universality, can be found in Corinthians I.3.9. We are all *theou sunergoi*, God's coworkers. This is a magnificent maxim. Where the figure of the master breaks down come those of the worker and of equality, conjoined. All equality is that of belonging together to a work. Indubitably, those participating in a truth procedure are coworkers in its becoming. This is what the metaphor of the son designates: a son is he whom an event relieves of the law and everything related to it for the benefit of a shared egalitarian endeavor.

It is nevertheless necessary to return to the event, upon which everything depends, and particularly the sons, coworkers in the enterprise of Truth. What must the event be for universality and equality to belong together under the aegis of the universal son?

For Paul, the event is certainly not the biography, teachings, recounting of miracles, aphorisms with a double meaning, of a particular individual: to wit, Jesus. The rule that applies to the divided Christian subject, and which privileges the active real of the declaration over private illumination, impersonal faith over particular exploits, also applies to Jesus. In the case of the latter, Paul, once again, will not deny that the Son enjoyed internal communication with the divine, that he was inhabited by unutterable utterances, and that, so far as miraculous cures, multiplication of loaves, walking on water, and other amazing feats are concerned, he was the equal of any of the charlatans that abounded in the empire's eastern provinces. He simply reminds us, even if only by deliberately neglecting to mention these extraneous virtuosities, that none of this is enough to found a new era of Truth. What the particular individual named Jesus said and did is only the contingent material seized upon by the event in view of an entirely different destiny. In this sense, Jesus is neither a master nor an example. He is the name for what happens to us universally.

Nietzsche, for whom Paul approaches the gospel accounts with "the cynicism of a rabbi," perfectly perceived the apostle's complete indifference to the anecdotal gentleness with which these accounts are filled. For Nietzsche, this is an instance of deliberate falsification, one wherein the hatred of life and the lust for power are given free rein:

The life, the example, the teaching, the death, the meaning and the right of the entire Gospel—nothing was left once this hate-obsessed counterfeiter had grasped what alone he could make us of. *Not* the reality, *not* the historical truth! . . . Paul simply shifted the centre of gravity of that entire existence *beyond* this existence—into the *lie* of the "resurrected" Jesus. In fact, he could make no use at all of the redeemer's life—he needed the death on the Cross *and* something in addition. (*The Anti-Christ*, §42)

This is not inaccurate. Like every genuine theoretician of truth, Paul, as we have seen, does not believe that there can be a "historical truth." Or rather, he does not believe truth to be a matter of history, of witnessing, of memory. Nietzsche, for his part, did not believe it either, for his genealogical doctrine is in no way historical. And it is true that, in Paul's eyes, without the motif of the Resurrection, Christ's existence would have been of little more importance than that of any other Oriental mystic, however talented.

But Nietzsche is not precise enough. When he writes that Paul needs only Christ's death "and something in addition," he should emphasize that this "something" is not "in addition" to death, that it is for Paul the unique point of the real onto which his thought fastens. And thus that, if he "shifted the center of gravity of that [Christ's] entire existence beyond this existence," it is neither in accordance with death, nor in accordance with hate, but in accordance with a principle of overexistence on the basis of which life, affirmative life, was restored and re-founded for all.

Does not Nietzsche himself want to "shift the center of gravity" of men's life beyond their contemporary nihilist decadence? And does he not require for this operation three closely related themes of which Paul is the inventor: to wit, that of the self-legitimating subjective declaration (the character of Zarathustra), the breaking of History in two ("grand politics"), and the new man as the end of guilty slavery and affirmation of life (the Overman)? If Nietzsche is so violent toward Paul, it is because he is his rival far more than his opponent. The result being that he "falsifies" Paul at least as much as, if not more than, Paul "falsified" Jesus.

To say that Paul shifted "the center of gravity of life out of life into the 'Beyond'—into Nothingness," and that in so doing he "deprived life as such of its centre of gravity" (*The Anti-Christ*, §43), is to maintain the very opposite of the apostle's teaching, for whom it is here and now that life takes revenges on death, here and now that we can live affirmatively, according to the spirit, rather than negatively, according to the flesh, which is the thought of death. For Paul, the Resurrection is that on the basis of which life's center of gravity resides in life, whereas previously, being situated in the Law, it organized life's subsumption by death.

In reality, the core of the problem is that Nietzsche harbors a genuine loathing for universalism. Not always: this mad saint is a violent living contradiction, a breaking in two of himself. But where Paul is concerned, yes: "The poison of the doctrine 'equal rights for all'—this has been more thoroughly sowed by Christianity than by anything else" (*The Anti-Christ*, §43). Where God is concerned, Nietzsche extols the virtues of the most obstinate particularism, the most unbridled racial communitarianism: "Formerly he [God] represented a people, the strength of a people, everything aggressive and thirsting for power in the soul of a people. . . . There is in fact no other alternative for Gods: either they are the will to power—and so long as they are that they will be national Gods— or else the impotence for power" (*The Anti-Christ*, §16). What Nietzsche—on this point remaining a German "mythologue" (in Lacoue-Labarthe's sense of the term)—cannot forgive Paul for is not so much to have willed Nothingness, but to have rid us of these sinister "national Gods" and to have formulated a theory of a subject who, as Nietzsche admirably, albeit disgustedly, puts it, is universally, "a rebel . . . against everything privileged" (*The Anti-Christ*, §46).

Moreover, while protesting against Paul in the name of "historical truth," Nietzsche does not seem to have appropriately situated the apostle's preaching relative to the canonical shaping of the gospel narratives. He pays little attention to the fact that these narratives, wherein he claims to discern the "psychology of the Redeemer" (a Buddha of decadence, a partisan of the quiet, empty life, "the last man"), were composed and organized long after Paul fiercely seized upon the only point that is supernumerary relative to this "Buddhist" edification: the Resurrection.

But nothing is more indispensable than to keep in mind the temporal relation between the synoptic Gospels, in which the edifying anecdote is essential, and Paul's epistles, charged from beginning to end with the revolutionary announcement of a spiritual history that has been broken in two. The Gospels literally come twenty years later. The Pauline reference is of a different substance. The event is not a teaching; Christ is not a master; disciples are out of the question. Jesus is certainly "lord" (*kurios*), and Paul his "servant" (*doulos*). But the Christ-event establishes the authority of a new subjective path over future eras. The fact that we must serve a truth procedure is not to be confused with slavery, which is precisely that from which we are forever released insofar as we all become sons of what has happened to us. The relation between lord and servant differs absolutely from that between master and disciple, as well as from that between owner and slave. It is not a relation of personal, or legal, dependence. It is a community of destiny in that moment in which we have to become a "new creature." That is why we need retain of Christ only what ordains this destiny, which is indifferent to the particularities of the living person: Jesus is resurrected; nothing else matters, so that Jesus becomes like an anonymous variable, a "someone" devoid of predicative traits, entirely absorbed by his resurrection.

The pure event is reducible to this: Jesus died on the cross and resurrected. This event is "grace" (*kharis*). Thus, it is neither a bequest, nor a tradition, nor a teaching. It is supernumerary relative to all this and presents itself as pure givenness.

As subject to the ordeal of the real, we are henceforth constituted by evental grace. The crucial formula—which, it must be noted, is simultaneously a universal address—is: *ou gar este hupo nomon all' hupo kharin*, "for you are not under law, but under grace" (Rom. 6.14). A structuring of the subject according to a "not . . . but" through which it must be understood as a becoming rather than a state. For the "not being under law" negatively indicates the path of the flesh as suspension of the subject's destiny, while "being under grace" indicates the path of the spirit as fidelity to the event. The subject of the new epoch is a "not . . . but." The event is at once the suspension of the path of the flesh through a problematic "not," and the affirmation of the path of the spirit through a "but" of exception. Law and grace are for the subject the name of the constituting weave through which he is related to the situation as it is and to the effects of the event as they have to become.

We shall maintain, in effect, that an evental rupture always constitutes its subject in the divided form of a "not . . . but," and that *it is precisely this form that bears the universal.* For the "not" is the potential dissolution of closed particularities (whose name is "law"), while the "but" indicates the task, the faithful labor, in which the subjects of the process opened up by the event (whose name is "grace") are the coworkers. The universal is neither on the side of the flesh as conventional lawfulness and particular state of the world, nor on the side of the pure spirit, as private inhabitation by grace and truth. The Jewish discourse of the rite and the law is undermined by the event's superabundance, but, equally, the arrogant discourse of internal revelation and the unutterable is abolished. The second and fourth discourses must be revoked because they *unify* the subject. Only the third discourse holds to its division as a guarantee of universality. If the event is able to enter into the constitution of the subject declaring it, it is precisely because through it, and irrespective of the particularity of persons, it ceaselessly redivides the two paths, distributing the "not . . . but," which, through an endless process, sets aside the law the better to enter into grace.

6

The Antidialectic of Death and Resurrection

We said: the event consists in Jesus, the Christ, dying on the cross and coming back to life. What is death's function in this affair? Does Paul's thought ultimately constitute, as Nietzsche believed, a moribund paradigm, an eventalization of the hatred of life?

Or again: Is the Pauline conception of the event dialectical? Is the path of affirmation always that of the labor of the negative, so that "the life of the spirit is the life that withstands death and maintains itself in it"? We know how much the Hegelian apparatus owes to Christianity, and how dialectical philosophy incorporates the theme of a Calvary of the Absolute. In that case, resurrection is nothing but the negation of the negation, death is the decisive time of the Infinite's self-externalization, and suffering and martyrdom possess an intrinsically redemptive function, which, it has to be said, corresponds to a Christian imagery that has been omnipresent for centuries.

If the theme of resurrection becomes caught up in the dialectical apparatus, it must be conceded that the event as supernumerary givenness and incalculable grace is dissolved into an auto-foundational and necessarily deployed rational protocol. It is certainly true that Hegelian philosophy, which is the rational edge of German romanticism, effects a capture of the Christ-event. In Hegel, grace becomes a moment in the self-development of the Absolute, and the material of death and suffering is the due required so that spirituality, externalizing itself in finitude, can return into itself through the experienced intensity of self-consciousness.

I shall maintain that Paul's position is antidialectical, and that for it death is in no way the obligatory exercise of the negative's immanent power. Grace, consequently, is not a "moment" of the Absolute. It is affirmation without preliminary negation; it is what comes upon us in caesura of the law. It is pure and simple *encounter*.

This de-dialectization of the Christ-event allows us to extract a formal, wholly secularized conception of grace from the mythological core. Everything hinges on knowing whether an ordinary existence, breaking with time's cruel routine, encounters the material chance of serving a truth, thereby becoming, through subjective division and beyond the human animal's survival imperatives, an immortal.

If Paul helps us to seize the link between evental grace and the universality of the True, it is so that we can tear the lexicon of grace and encounter away from its religious confinement. That materialism is never anything but the ideology of the determination of the subjective by the objective disqualified it philosophically. Or let us posit that it is incumbent upon us to found a materialism of grace through the strong, simple idea that every existence can one day be seized by what happens to it and subsequently devote itself to that which is valid for all, or as Paul magnificently puts it, "become all things to all men [*tois pasi gegona ta panta*]" (Cor. I.9.22).

Yes, we are the beneficiaries of certain graces, ones for which there is no need to invoke an All-Powerful.

For Paul himself, who certainly upholds and exalts the transcendent machinery, the event is not death, it is resurrection.

Let us, on this delicate point, provide a few indications.

Suffering plays no role in Paul's apologetic, not even in the case of Christ's death. The weak, abject character of that death is certainly important for him, insofar as the treasure of the event—we have already said why—has to reside in an earthen vessel. But for Paul, that the force of a truth is immanent to that which is weakness and folly so far as the established discourses are concerned, never entails that suffering possesses an intrinsically redemptive function. The share of suffering is inevitable; such is the law of the world. But hope, wagered by the event and the subject who binds himself to it, distributes consolation as that suffering's only real, here and now: "Or hope for you is unshaken, for we know that as you share in our sufferings, you will also share in our consolation" (Cor. II.1.7). In fact, the glory tied to the thought of "invisible things" is incommensurable with the inevitable sufferings inflicted by the ordinary world: "For these slight momentary afflictions are preparing for us an eternal weight of glory beyond all comparison" (Cor. II.4.17).

When Paul speaks of his own sufferings it is in accordance with a strictly militant logic. It is a matter of convincing dissident groups, or ones tempted by the adversary, that he, Paul, is well and truly the risk-taking, disinterested man of action he claims to be. This is particularly so in the second epistle to the Corinthians, marked by a very noticeable political anxiety, in which Paul alternates flattery and threats ("I beg of you that when I am present I may not have to show boldness with such confidence as I count on showing against some" [Cor. II.10.2]). At this point, deployed as part of a tactic in which pleas are combined with rivalry, there comes the powerful description of the hardships endured by the nomadic leader:

Often near death, five times I have received at the hands of the Jews the forty lashes less one. Three times I have been beaten with rods; once I was stoned. Three times I have been shipwrecked; a night and a day I have been adrift at sea; on frequent journeys, in danger from rivers, danger from robbers . . . danger in the city, danger in the wilderness, danger at sea, danger from false brethren, in toil and hardship, through many a sleepless night, in hunger and thirst, often without food, in cold and exposure. (Cor. II.11.23–27)

But the conclusion of this biographical passage, entirely designed to confound those who "when they measure themselves by one another and compare themselves with one another, are without understanding" (Cor. II.10.12), ascribes no redemptive signification to the apostle's tribulations. Here again, as always, it is a question of the earthen vessel, of the postevental bearing of weakness, of the destitution of the worldly criteria of glory: "If I must glory, I will glory in the things that show my weakness" (Cor. II.11.30).

Let us propose the formula: in Paul, there is certainly the Cross, but no path of the Cross. There is Calvary, but no ascent to Calvary. Energetic and urgent, Paul's preaching includes no masochistic propaganda extolling the virtues of suffering, no pathos of the crown of thorns, flagellation, oozing blood, or the gall-soaked sponge.

We come now to the Cross.

For Paul, death cannot be the operation of salvation. For it is on the side of flesh and the law. It is, as we have seen, the configuration of the real through the subjective path of the flesh. Not only has it no sacred function, no spiritual assignation; it cannot have one.

To understand its function, it is once more necessary to forget the Platonic apparatus of the soul and the body, of the soul's survival, or its immortality. Paul's thought ignores these parameters. The death about which Paul tells us, which is ours as much as Christ's, has nothing biological about it, no more so for that matter than life. Death and life are thoughts, interwoven dimensions of the global subject, wherein "body" and "soul" are indiscernible (which is why, for Paul, the Resurrection is necessarily resurrection of the body—that is to say, resurrection of the divided subject *in its entirety*). Grasped as thought, as subjective path, as way of being in the world, death is that part of the divided subject that must, again and always, say "no" to the flesh and maintain itself in the precarious becoming of the spirit's "but."

Death, which is the thought of (= according to) the flesh cannot be constitutive of the Christ-event. Death is, moreover, an Adamic phenomenon. It was, properly speaking, *invented* by Adam, the first man. Corinthians I.15.22 is perfectly clear on this point: "For as by a man came death, by a man has come also the resurrection of the dead. For as in Adam all die, so also in Christ shall all be made alive." Death is as ancient as the first man's choice of a rebellious freedom. What constitutes an event in Christ is exclusively the Resurrection, that *anastasis nekrōn* that should be translated as the raising up of the dead, their uprising, which is the uprising of life.

Why then must Christ die, and to what ends does Paul expand on the symbol of the cross?

In the text above, one must pay careful attention to the fact that only the resurrection of a man can in a certain sense accord with or be situated on the same level as the invention of death by a man. Christ invents life, but can do so only insofar as he, just like the inventor of death, is a man, a thought, an existence. Ultimately, Adam and Jesus, the first Adam and the second Adam, incarnate, at the scale of humanity's destiny, the subjective weave that composes, as constituting division, any singular subject whatsoever. Christ dies simply in order to attest that it well and truly is a man who, capable of inventing death, is also capable of inventing life. Or: Christ dies in order to manifest that, in spite of his also being caught up in the human invention of death, it is from this very point (indexing what humanity is capable of) that he invents life.

In sum, death is only required insofar as, with Christ, divine intervention must, in its very principle, become strictly equal to the humanity of man, and hence to the thought that dominates him, which as subject is called "flesh," and as object "death." When Christ dies, we, mankind, shall cease to be separated from God, since by filiating Himself with the sending of his Son, He enters into the most intimate proximity to our thinking composition.

Such is the unique necessity of Christ's death: it is the means to an equality with God himself. Through this thought of the flesh, whose real is death, is dispensed to us in grace the fact of being in the same element as God himself. Death here names a renunciation of transcendence. Let us say that Christ's death *sets up an immanentization of the spirit*.

Paul is perfectly aware that maintaining a radical transcendence of the Father allows neither the event, nor the rupture with the legal order. For only the deathly immobility of the Law, that "minister of death, carved in letters on stone" (Cor. II.3.7), can occupy the abyss separating us from God.

In Romans 6.4–9, Paul establishes that a doctrine of the real as event has conditions of immanence, and that we can enter into relation with death only insofar as God enters into relation with it. The operation of death thereby constructs the site of our divine equality within humanity itself:

We were buried therefore with him by baptism into death, so that as Christ was raised from the dead by the glory of the Father, we too might walk in newness of life.

For if we have been united with him in a death like his, we shall certainly be united with him in a resurrection like his. We know that our old self was crucified with him so that the sinful body might be destroyed, and we might no longer be enslaved to sin. For he who has died is free from sin. But if we have died with Christ, we believe that we shall also live with him. For we know that Christ being raised from the dead will never die again.

The text is explicit: death as such counts for nothing in the operation of salvation. It functions as a condition of immanence. We conform to Christ insofar as he conforms to us. The cross (we have been crucified with Christ) is the symbol of that identity. And this conformity is possible because death is not a biological fact but a thought of the flesh, one of whose names—an extremely complex one, to which we shall come back—is "sin." Paul calls this immanentization a "reconciliation" (*katallagē*): "For if while we were enemies of God we were reconciled to him by the death of his Son, much more, now that we are reconciled, shall we be saved by his life" (Rom. 5.10).

It is imperative not to confuse *katallagē*, reconciliation, which is the operation of death, with *sōtēria*, salvation, which is the evental operation of resurrection. The former immanentizes the conditions of the latter without thereby rendering the latter necessary. Through Christ's death, God renounces his transcendent separation; he unseparates himself through filiation and shares in a constitutive dimension of the divided human subject. In so doing he creates, not the event, but what I call its site. The evental site is that datum that is immanent to a situation and enters into the composition of the event itself, addressing it to *this* singular situation, rather than another. Death is construction of the evental site insofar as it brings it about that resurrection (which cannot be inferred from it) *will have been* addressed to men, to their subjective situation. Reconciliation is a given of the site, a virtual indication—inoperative by itself—of the extent to which Christ's resurrection consists in the invention of a new life *by man*. Resurrection alone is a given of the event, which mobilizes the site and whose operation is salvation.

Ultimately, to understand the relation between *katallagē* and *sōtēria*, which is just as much the relation between death and life, is to understand that, for Paul, there is an absolute disjunction between Christ's death and his resurrection. For death is an operation in the situation, an operation that immanentizes the evental site, while resurrection is the event as such. Hence the fact that Paul's argument is foreign to all dialectics. Resurrection is neither a sublation, nor an overcoming of death. They are two distinct functions, whose articulation contains no necessity. For the event's sudden emergence never follows from the existence of an evental site. Although it requires conditions of immanence, that sudden emergence nevertheless remains of the order of grace.

This is why Nietzsche goes completely astray when he turns Paul into the archetypal priest, power subordinated to the hatred of life. We are all familiar with the diatribe:

Then Paul appeared. . . . Paul, Chandala hatred against Rome, against "the world," become flesh and genius, the Jew, the eternal Jew par excellence. . . . This was his vision on the road to Damascus: he grasped that to disvalue "the world" he needed the belief in immortality, that the concept "Hell" will master even Rome—that with the "Beyond" one kills life. . . . Nihilist and Christian: they rhyme, and do not merely rhyme. (*The Anti-Christ*, §58)

Nothing in this text fits. We have already said enough to understand that "belief in immortality" is no concern of Paul's, who would far rather see affirmation triumph over negation, life over death, the new man (the overman?) over the old man; that, in the case of a man who was particularly proud of his Roman citizenship, the hatred against Rome is Nietzsche's invention; that "the world" that Paul declares has been crucified with Jesus is the Greek cosmos, the reassuring totality that allots places and orders thought to consent to those places, and that it is consequently a question of letting in the vital rights of the infinite and the untotalizable event; that no mention is made of hell in Paul's preaching, and that it is a characteristic of his manner never to appeal to fear and always to courage; finally, that "to kill life" is certainly not the intent of he who asks with a sort of savage joy: "O death, where is thy victory?" (Cor. I.15.55). Paul's program would be better summarized by the formula "to kill death."

He who demanded Dionysian affirmation, him who, like Paul, believed himself to be breaking the history of the world in two, and to be everywhere substituting life's "yes" for nihilism's "no," would have found better inspiration by citing this passage:

For the Son of God, Jesus Christ, whom we preached among you, Silvanus and Timothy and I, was not Yes and No; but in him it is always Yes. (Cor. II.1.19)

This is what Paul is about: not the cult of death but the foundation of a universal "yes."

Similarly, he who wished that, beyond good and evil, beyond rites and priests, the new man, the overhumanity of which humanity is capable, might come forth, could have invoked Paul in his favor, the Paul who declares, in a very Nietzschean tone: "For neither circumcision counts for anything, nor uncircumcision, but being a new creature" (Gal. 6.15).

Nietzsche is Paul's rival far more than his opponent. Both share the same desire to initiate a new epoch in human history, the same conviction that man can and must be overcome, the same certainty that we must have done with guilt and law. Is he not Nietzsche's brother, the Paul who declares: "For if there was splendor in the dispensation of condemnation, the dispensation of righteousness must far exceed it in splendor" (Cor. II.3.9)? They share the same—sometimes brutal—combination of vehemence and saintly gentleness. The same touchiness. The same certainty as to being personally chosen. Nietzsche expounding the reasons why he is "a destiny" is the counterpart to the Paul who knows he has been "set apart for the gospel of God" (Rom. 1.1). And finally, they share the same universality of address, the same global wandering. In order to found a grand (and even, he says, a "very grand") politics, Nietzsche questions the resources of all peoples, declares himself Polish, wants to enter into alliance with the Jews, writes to Bismarck. . . . And in order not to become prisoner of any local group or provincial sect, Paul travels ideally throughout the empire and rebuts those who wish to pin him down with: "I am under obligation both to the Greeks and to barbarians, both to the wise and to the foolish" (Rom. 1.14).

The truth is that both brought antiphilosophy to the point where it no longer consists in a "critique," however radical, of the whims and pettinesses of the metaphysician or sage. A much more serious matter is at issue: that of bringing about through the event an unqualified affirmation of life against the reign of death and the negative. Of being he who, Paul or Zarathustra, anticipates without flinching the moment wherein "death is engulfed in victory" (Cor. I.15.54).

Despite being close to Nietzsche from this point of view, Paul is obviously not the dialectician he is sometimes taken to be. It is not a question of denying death by preserving it, but of engulfing it, abolishing it.

Neither is Paul, like the early Heidegger, a proponent of being-toward-death and finitude. In the divided subject, the part of being-toward-death is that which still says "no," that which does not want to let itself be carried away by the exceptional "but" of grace, of the event, of life.

Ultimately, for Paul, the Christ-event is nothing but resurrection. It eradicates negativity, and if, as we have already said, death is required for the construction of its site, it remains an affirmative operation that is irreducible to death itself.

Christ has been pulled *ek nekrōn*, out from the dead. This extraction from the mortal site establishes a point wherein death loses its power. Extraction, subtraction, but not negation: "But if we have died with Christ, we believe that we shall also live with him. For we know that Christ being raised from the dead will never die again; death no longer has dominion over him" (Rom. 6.8–9).

Death, as the Son's human site, is nothing but powerlessness when subjected to the eventral trial of resurrection. Resurrection suddenly comes forth *out from* the power of death, not through its negation.

One could say: the Christ-event, the fact of there having been this particular son, out from the power of death, retroactively identifies death as a path, a dimension of the subject, and not a state of affairs. Death is not a destiny but a choice, as is shown by the fact that we can be offered, through the subtraction of death, the choice of life. And thus, strictly speaking, there is no being-toward-death; there is only ever a path-of-death entering into the divided composition of every subject.

If resurrection is affirmative subtraction from the path of death, we have to understand why, in Paul's eyes, this—radically singular—event provides the basis for a universalism. What is it in this resurrection, this "out from the dead," that has the power to suspend differences? Why, if a man is resurrected, does it follow that there is neither Greek nor Jew, neither male nor female, neither slave nor free man?

The resurrected is what filiates us and includes itself in the generic dimension of the son. It is essential to remember that for Paul, Christ is not identical with God, that no Trinitarian or substantialist theology upholds his preaching. Wholly faithful to the pure event, Paul restricts himself to the metaphor of "the sending of the son." As a result, for Paul, it is not the infinite that died on the cross. Certainly, the construction of the evental site requires that the son who was sent to us, terminating the abyss of transcendence, be immanent to the path of the flesh, of death, to all the dimensions of the human subject. In no way does this entail that Christ is the incarnation of a God, or that he must be thought of as the becoming-finite of the infinite. *Paul's thought dissolves incarnation in resurrection.*

However, although resurrection is not the "Calvary of the Absolute," although it mobilizes no dialectic of the incarnation of Spirit, it is nevertheless true that it suspends differences for the benefit of a radical universality, and that the event is addressed to all without exception, or definitively divides every subject. This is precisely what, in terms of the Roman world, constitutes a staggering innovation. It can be illuminated only by scrutinizing the names of death and the names of life. First among the names of death, however, is Law.

7

Paul Against the Law

Two statements seem jointly to concentrate, in a perilous metonymy, Paul's teaching:

1. Faith is what saves us, not works.
2. We are no longer under the rule of law, but of grace.

There would thus seem to be four concepts coordinating a subject's fundamental choices: *pistis* (faith) and *ergon* (work); *kharis* (grace) and *nomos* (law). The subjective path of the flesh (*sarx*), whose real is death, coordinates the pairing of law and works. While the path of the spirit (*pneuma*), whose real is life, coordinates that of grace and faith. Between the two lies the new real object, the eventual given, traversing "the redemption which is in Christ Jesus," passing through *dia tēs apolutrōseōs tēs en Khristōi Iēsou* (Rom. 3.24).

But why is it necessary to reject law onto the side of death? Because considered in its particularity, that of the works it prescribes, the law blocks the subjectivation of grace's universal address as pure conviction, or faith. The law "objectifies" salvation and forbids one from relating it to the gratuitousness of the Christ-event. In Romans 3.27–30, Paul clearly indicates what is at issue, which is the essential link between event and universality when it is a question of the One, or more simply of *one* truth:

Then what becomes of our boasting? It is excluded. On what principle? On the principle of works? No, but on the principle of faith. For we hold that a man is justified by faith apart from works of law. Or is God the God of the Jews only? Is he not the God of Gentiles also? Yes, of Gentiles also, since God is one; and he will justify the circumcised on the grounds of their faith and the uncircumcised through their faith.

The fundamental question is that of knowing precisely what it means for there to be a single God. What does the "mono" in "monotheism" mean? Here Paul confronts—but also renews the terms of—the formidable question of the One. His genuinely revolutionary conviction is that *the sign of the One is the "for all," or the "without exception."* That there is but a single God must be understood not as a philosophical speculation concerning substance or the supreme being, but on the basis of a structure of address. The One is that which inscribes no difference in the subjects to which it addresses itself. The One is only insofar as it is for all: such is the maxim of universality when it has its root in the event. Monotheism can be understood only by taking into consideration the whole of humanity. Unless addressed to all, the One crumbles and disappears.

But, for Paul, the law always designates a particularity, hence a difference. It is not possible for it to be an operation of the One, because it addresses its fallacious "One" only to those who acknowledge and practice the injunctions it specifies.

The ontological structure underlying this conviction (though Paul has no interest whatsoever in ontology) is that no evental One can be the One of a particularity. The universal is the only possible correlate for the One. The general apparatus of a truth contains the One (divine transcendence, monotheism, according to the Pauline fable), the universal (the whole of humanity, both circumcised and uncircumcised), and the singular (the Christ-event). The particular, which pertains to opinion, custom, law, cannot be inscribed in it.

What can measure up to the universality of an address? Not legality, in any case. The law is always predicative, particular, and partial. Paul is perfectly aware of the law's unfailingly "statist" character. By "statist" I mean that which enumerates, names, and controls the parts of a situation. If a truth is to surge forth eventally, it must be nondenumerable, impredicable, uncontrollable. This is precisely what Paul calls grace: that which occurs without being couched in any predicate, that which is translegal, that which happens to everyone without an assignable reason. Grace is the opposite of law insofar as it is what comes *without being due.*

This is a profound insight of Paul's, which, through its universal and illegal understanding of the One, undoes every particular or communitarian incorporation of the subject, as well as every juridical or contractual approach to its constitutive division. *That which founds a subject cannot be what is due to it.* For this foundation binds itself to that which is declared in a radical contingency. If one understands man's humanity in terms of his subjective capacity, there is, strictly speaking, nothing whatsoever like a "right" of man.

The polemic against the "what is due," against the logic of right and duty, lies at the heart of the Pauline refusal of works and law: "To one who works, his wages are not reckoned as a grace but as his due" (Rom. 4.4). But for Paul, nothing is due. The salvation of the subject cannot take the form of a reward or wage. The subjectivity of faith is unwaged (which, in the final analysis, entitles us to call it communist). It pertains to the granting of a gift, *kharisma.* Every subject is initiated on the basis of a charisma; every subject is charismatic. Since the subjectivating point is the declaration of the event, rather than the work that demands a wage or reward, the declaring subject exists according to the charisma proper to him. Every subjectivity confronts its division within the element of an essential gratuitousness proper to its purpose. The redemptive operation consists in the occurrence of a charisma.

There is in Paul a fundamental link between universalism and charisma, between the One's universal power of address, and the absolute gratuitousness of militantism. Thus, in Romans 3.22–24, he will state: "For there is no distinction [*diastolē*, which means "difference"], since all have sinned and fall short of the glory of God, by his grace they are justified as a gift [*dōrean*], through the redemption which is in Christ Jesus."

Dōrean is a powerful word; it means "as a pure gift," "without cause," and even "in vain." There is for Paul an essential link between the "for all" of the universal and the "without cause." There is an address for all only according to that which is without cause. Only what is absolutely gratuitous can be addressed to all. Only charisma and grace measure up to a universal problem.

The subject constituted by charisma through the gratuitous practice of the universal address necessarily maintains that there are no differences. Only what is charismatic, thus absolutely without cause, possesses this power of being in excess of the law, of collapsing established differences.

This is the root of the famous Pauline theme concerning the superabundance of grace. The law governs a predicative, worldly multiplicity, granting to each part of the whole its due. Evental grace governs a multiplicity in excess of itself, one that is indescribable, superabundant relative to itself as well as with respect to the fixed distributions of the law.

The profound ontological thesis here is that universalism supposes one be able to think the multiple not as a part, but as in excess of itself, as that which is out of place, as a nomadism of gratuitousness. If by "sin" one understands the subjective exercise of death as path of existence, and hence the legal cult of particularity, one thereby understands that what is maintained of the event (which is to say, a truth, whatever it may be) is always in impredicable excess of everything circumscribed by "sin." This is precisely what is said by the famous text of Romans 5.20–21:

Law came in, to increase the trespass; but where sin increased, grace abounded all the more, so that, as sin reigned in death, grace also might reign through righteousness to eternal life through Jesus Christ, our Lord.

The two subjective paths, death and life, whose nonrelation constitutes the divided subject, are also two types of multiplicity:

> • The particularizing multiplicity, the one accompanied by its own limit, marked by the predicate of its limit. The law is its cipher or letter.

> • The multiplicity that, exceeding itself, upholds universality. Its being in excess of itself precludes its being represented as a totality. Superabundance cannot be assigned to any Whole. That is precisely why it legitimates the destitution of difference, a destitution that is the very process of excess.

What is called "grace" is the capacity of a postevental multiplicity to exceed its own limit, a limit that has a commandment of the law as its dead cipher. The opposition grace/law encompasses two doctrines of the multiple.

It remains to be understood why the subjective theme associated with law is that of sin. Here we face an extremely complex intrigue. Nevertheless, what entails that "law" is henceforth one of the names of death in subjective composition.

In fact, what is at issue is desire (*epithumia*), which there is no reason to translate here by a "concupiscence" that has far too strong a whiff of the confessional about it. Before proceeding onto the subject's "new life," the most profound grasp of the connections between desire, law, death, and life is necessary.

Paul's fundamental thesis is that the law, and only the law, endows desire with an autonomy sufficient for the subject of this desire, from the perspective of that autonomy, to come to occupy the place of the dead.

The law is what gives life to desire. But in so doing, it constrains the subject so that he wants to follow only the path of death.

What is sin exactly? It is not desire as such, for if it were one would not understand its link to the law and death. *Sin is the life of desire as autonomy, as automatism.* The law is required in order to unleash the automatic life of desire, the automatism of repetition. For only the law *fixes* the object of desire, binding desire to it regardless of the subject's "will." It is this objectal automatism of desire, inconceivable without the law, that assigns the subject to the carnal path of death.

Clearly, what is at issue here is nothing less than the problem of the unconscious (Paul calls it the involuntary, what I do not want, *ho ou thelō*). The life of desire fixed and unleashed by the law is that which, decentered from the subject, accomplishes itself as unconscious automatism, with respect to which the involuntary subject is capable only of inventing death.

The law is what, by designating its object, delivers desire to its repetitive autonomy. Desire thereby attains its automatism in the form of a transgression. How are we to understand "transgression"? There is transgression when what is prohibited—which is to say, negatively named by the law—becomes the object of a desire that lives through itself in the site and place of the subject. Paul condenses this intersecting of the imperative, desire, and subjective death, thus: "For sin, finding opportunity in the commandment, seduced me and by it killed me" (Rom. 7.11).

Difficult to imagine a more anti-Kantian disposition than the one which, by calling the autonomy of desire "sin" when its object is fixed by the law's commandment, designates the effect of the latter as the subject's coming to occupy the place of the dead.

Up to now we have been anticipating. But everything is spelled out in what is perhaps Paul's most famous, yet also most intricate text, Romans 7.7–23, a text I will cite in its entirety before carrying on with its elucidation.

What then shall we say? That the Law is sin? By no means! Yet if it had not been for the Law, I should not have known sin. I should not have known what it is to covet if the Law had not said, "You shall not covet." But sin, finding opportunity in the commandment, wrought in me all kinds of covetousness. Apart from the Law sin lies dead. I was once alive apart from the Law, but when the commandment came, sin revived and I died; the very commandment that promised life proved to be death to me. For sin, finding opportunity in the commandment, seduced me and by it killed me. So the Law is holy, and the commandment is holy and just and good.

Did that which is good, then, bring death to me? By no means! It was sin, working death in me through what is good, in order that sin might be shown to be sin, and through the commandment might become sinful beyond measure. We know that the Law is spiritual; but I am carnal, sold under sin. I do not understand my own actions. For I do not do what I want, but I do the very thing I hate. Now, if I do what I do not want, I agree that the Law is good. So then it is no longer I that do it, but sin which dwells within me. For I know that nothing good dwells within me, that is, in my flesh. I can will what is right, but I cannot do it. For I do not do the good I want, but the evil I do not want is what I do. Now if I do what I do not want, it is no longer I that do it, but sin which dwells in me.

So I find it to be a law that when I want to do right, evil lies close at hand. For I delight in the law of God, in my inmost self, but I see in my members another law at war with the law of my mind and making me captive to the law of sin that dwells in my members.

All of Paul's thinking here points toward a theory of the subjective unconscious, structured through the opposition life/death. The law's prohibition is that through which the desire of the object can realize itself "involuntarily," unconsciously—which is to say, as life of sin. As a result of which the subject, de-centered from this desire, crosses over to the side of death.

What matters to Paul is that this experience (he is manifestly speaking about himself, almost in the style of Augustine's *Confessions*) causes to appear, under condition of the law, a singular disposition, wherein, if the subject is on the side of death, life is on the side of sin.

If the subject is to swing over into another disposition, one wherein he would be on the side of life, and sin—that is to say, the automatism of repetition—would occupy the place of the dead, it is necessary to break with the law. Such is Paul's implacable conclusion.

How is the subject of a universal truth structured, once his division is no longer sustained by law? Resurrection summons the subject to identify himself as such according to the name of faith (*pistis*). This means: independently of the results, or prescribed forms, that will be called works. In the guise of the event, the subject *is* subjectivation. The word *pistis* (faith, or conviction) designates precisely this point: the absence of any gap between subject and subjectivation. In this absence of a gap, which constantly activates the subject in the service of truth, forbidding him rest, the One-truth proceeds in the direction of all.

But perhaps we can, at this particular juncture, recapitulating and generalizing the figures occasioned in Paul by the virulence of the fable, arrange what is imbued with a materialist import by means of two theorems and thus delineate our materialism of grace.

Theorem 1. The One is only insofar as it is for all, and follows not from the law, but from the event.

It is in the retroaction of the event that the universality of a truth is constituted. The law is inappropriate to the "for all" because it is always the statist law, the law that controls parts, the particular law. The One *is* only in default of the law. Universality is organically bound to the contingency of what happens to us, which is the senseless superabundance of grace.

Theorem 2. It is the event alone, as illegal contingency, which causes a multiplicity in excess of itself to come forth and thus allows for the possibility of overstepping finitude. The subjective corollary, perfectly established by Paul, is that every law is the cipher of a finitude. This is precisely what entails that it bind itself to the path of the flesh and, ultimately, death. That which prohibits monotheism by particularizing its address, also prohibits the infinite.

But let us, for a moment more, pursue the labyrinth of the epistle to the Romans.

We have already pointed it out in the text: without the law, there is no liberated, autonomous, automatic desire. There is an indistinct, undivided life, perhaps something like Adamic life, before the fall, before the law. Paul is invoking a kind of infancy when he says: "Once I was alive apart from the Law." For this "life" is not the one that constitutes the entire real that belongs to the path of the spirit in the divided subject. Rather, it is a life that unseparates the two paths, the life of a subject who is supposed as full, or undivided. If one supposes that there is this "before" of the law, one supposes an innocent subject, one who has not even invented death. Or rather, death is on the side of desire: "Apart from the law sin lies dead." This means: apart from the law, there is no living autonomy of desire. In the indistinct subject, desire remains an empty, inactive category. That which will later be the path of death, or that which makes the subject swing over into the place of the dead, is not living. "Before the law," the path of death is dead. But by the same token, this innocent life remains foreign to the question of salvation.

"With the law," the subject has definitively exited from unity, from innocence. His putative indistinction can no longer be maintained. Desire, whose object is designated by the law, finds itself determined—autonomized—as transgressive desire. With the law, desire regains life; it becomes a full, active category. There is a constitution of the carnal path thanks to the objectal multiplicity that the law carves out through prohibition and nomination. Sin appears as the automation of desire.

But the path of sin is that of death. Consequently, it becomes possible to say that (and this lies at the heart of Paul's discourse) *with the law, the path of death, which was itself dead, becomes alive once more.* The law gives life to death, and the subject as life according to the spirit falls onto the side of death. The law distributes life on the side of the path of death, and death on the side of the path of life.

The death of life is the Self (in the position of the dead). The life of death is sin.

Note the powerful paradox in this disjunction between (dead) Self and (living) sin. It signifies that it is never I who sin, it is sin that sins in me: "Sin took hold of me through the commandment and by it killed me." And "It is no longer I who act, but the sin that inhabits me." Sin as such does not interest Paul, who is everything except a moralist. What counts is its subjective position, its genealogy. Sin is the life of death. It is that of which the law, and the law alone, is capable. The price paid for this is that life occupies the place of the dead under the auspices of the Self.

The extreme tension running through this text comes from the fact that Paul is striving to articulate a de-centering of the subject, a particularly contorted form of its division. Since the subject of life is in the place of death and vice versa, it follows that knowledge and will, on the one hand, agency and action, on the other, are entirely disconnected. This is the empirically verifiable essence of existence according to the law. Moreover, a parallel can be drawn between this de-centering and the Lacanian interpretation of the cogito (there where I think, I am not, and there where I am, I do not think).

Let us generalize a little. For Paul, the man of the law is one in whom doing is separated from thinking. Such is the consequence of seduction by commandment. This figure of the subject, wherein the division lies between the dead Self and the involuntary automation of living desire, is, for thought, a figure of powerlessness. Basically, sin is not so much a fault as living thought's inability to prescribe action. Under the effect of the law, thought disintegrates into powerlessness and endless cogitation, because the subject (the dead Self) is disconnected from a limitless power: that of desire's living automation.

Accordingly, we will posit that:

Theorem 3. The law is what constitutes the subject as powerlessness of thought.

But the law consists above all in the letter's force of commandment. The terrible formula in Corinthians II.3.6 is well known: *to gramma apoktennei, to de pneuma zōopoiei,* "the letter kills, but the spirit gives life." It is followed by a mention of "the dispensation of death, carved in letters on stone" (Cor. II.3.7). The letter mortifies the subject insofar as it separates his thought from all power.

We shall define "salvation" (Paul says: justified life, or justification) thus: that thought can be unseparated from doing and power. There is salvation when the divided figure of the subject maintains thought in the power of doing. This is what, for my part, I call a truth procedure.

Accordingly, we have:

Theorem 4. There is no letter of salvation, or literal form for a truth procedure.

This means that there can be a letter only of automatism, of calculation. The corollary follows: there is calculation only of the letter. There is a reckoning only of death. Every letter is blind and operates blindly.

When the subject is under the letter, or literal, he presents himself as a disconnected correlation between an automatism of doing and a powerlessness of thought.

If one defines "salvation" as the ruin of this disjunction, it is clear that it will depend on a lawless eruption, unchaining the point of powerlessness from automatism.

It is important to understand and recapitulate the antidialectic of salvation and sin. Salvation is the unchaining of the subjective figure whose name is sin. We have seen, in effect, that sin is a subjective structure, and not an evil act. Sin is nothing but the permutation of the places of life and death under the effect of the law, which is precisely why Paul, dispensing with the need for a sophisticated doctrine of original sin, can simply say: we *are* in sin. When salvation unblocks the subjective mechanism of sin, it becomes apparent that this unchaining consists in a deliteralization of the subject.

This deliteralization is conceivable only if one admits that one of the paths of the divided subject is transliteral. So long as we are "under the law," this path remains dead (it is in the posture of the Self). Resurrection alone allows it to become active once more. The extrication of death and life, in the case where life occupied the position of death's remainder, becomes perceptible solely on the basis of the excess of grace, thus, of a pure act.

"Grace" means that thought cannot *wholly* account for the brutal starting over on the path of life in the subject, which is to say, for the rediscovered conjunction between thinking and doing. Thought can be raised up from its powerlessness only through something that exceeds the order of thought. "Grace" names the event as condition for an active thought. The condition is itself inevitably in excess of what it conditions, which is to say that grace is partly subtracted from the thought that it gives life to. Or, as Mallarmé—that Paul of the modern poem—will put it: it is certain that every thought emits a dice-throw, but it is just as certain that it will be unable to ultimately think the chance that has thus engendered it.

For Paul, the figure of the chiasmus death/life, coordinated by the law, can be raised up, which is to say, permutated once again, only through an implacable operation bearing on death and life, and this operation is resurrection. Only a resurrection redistributes death and life to their places, by showing that life does not necessarily occupy the place of the dead.

8

Love as Universal Power

It has been established that no morality—if one understands by "morality" practical obedience to a law—can justify the existence of a subject: "A man is not justified by works of the law but through faith in Jesus Christ" (Gal. 2.16). What is more, the Christ-event is essentially the abolition of the law, which was nothing but the empire of death: "Christ redeemed us from the curse of the law" (Gal. 3.13). Just as, under the law, the subject, de-centered from the automatic life of desire, occupied the place of the dead, and sin (or unconscious desire) enjoyed an autonomous life in him, similarly, having been sprung from death by resurrection, the subject participates in a new life, whose name is Christ. Christ's resurrection is just as much our resurrection, shattering that death wherein the subject, under the law, had exiled himself in the closed form of the Self: "If I live, it is no longer I who live, but Christ who lives in me" (Gal. 2.20). By the same token, if one persists in supposing that truth and justice can be obtained by observing legal commandments, one must return toward death, assert that no grace has been accorded us in existence, and deny the Resurrection: "I do not nullify the grace of God; for if justification [*dikaiosunē*] were through the law, then Christ died to no purpose" (Gal. 2.21).

Is this to say that the subject who binds himself to Christian discourse is absolutely *lawless*? In the passage of the epistle to the Romans that we examined at length, various clues point toward the opposite, obliging us to raise the extraordinarily difficult question concerning *the existence of a transliteral law, a law of the spirit.*

For at the very moment in which he sets out to depose the law and elucidate its relation to unconscious avidity, Paul points out that "the law is holy, and the commandment is holy and just and good [*hē entolē hagia kai dikaia kai agathē*]" (Rom. 7.12). What is more, apparently overturning at a stroke all of the foregoing dialectic, he asserts that "the law is spiritual [*ho nomos pneumatikos*]" (Rom. 7.14).

Thus, it seems necessary to distinguish between a legalizing subjectivation, which is a power of death, and a law raised up by faith, which belongs to the spirit and to life.

Our task consists in thinking the apparent contradiction between two statements:

1. "Christ is the end of the law [*telos nomou Khristos*]" (Rom. 10.4).
2. "Love is the fulfilling of the law [*plērōma nomou hē agapē*]" (Rom. 13.10).

Under the condition of faith, of a declared conviction, love names a nonliteral law, one that gives to the faithful subject his consistency, and effectuates the postevental truth in the world.

This, from my point of view, is a thesis endowed with a general relevance. The trajectory of a truth, which institutes its subject as detached from the statist laws of the situation, is nonetheless consistent according to another law: the one that, addressing the truth to everyone, universalizes the subject.

Theorem 5. A subject turns the universal address of the truth whose procedure he maintains into a nonliteral law.

To this universal address that faith, or pure subjectivation, does not constitute on its own Paul gives the name "love," *agapē*—translated for a long time as "charity," a term that no longer means much to us.

Its principle is this: when the subject as thought accords with the grace of the event—this is subjectivation (faith, conviction)—he, who was dead, returns to the place of life. He regains those attributes of power that had fallen onto the side of the law and whose subjective figure was sin. He rediscovers the living unity of thinking and doing. This recovery turns life itself into a universal law. Law returns as life's articulation for everyone, path of faith, law beyond law. This is what Paul calls love.

We already know that faith cannot be confused with mere private conviction, which, as we have seen, when left to itself, coordinates the fourth discourse, that of unutterable utterances, the enclosure of the mystical subject, rather than Christian discourse. Genuine subjectivation has as its material evidence the *public declaration* of the event by its name, which is "resurrection." It is of the essence of faith to publicly declare itself. Truth is either militant or is not. Citing Deuteronomy, Paul reminds us that "The word is near you, on your lips, and in your heart" (Rom. 10.8). And certainly, private conviction, that of the heart, is required, but only the public confession of faith installs the subject in the perspective of salvation. It is not the heart that saves, but the lips:

It is the word of faith we preach. If you confess with your lips that Jesus is Lord and believe in your heart that God raised him from the dead, you will be saved. For man believes with his heart and so is justified, and he confesses with his lips and so is saved (Rom. 10.9–10).

The real of faith is an effective declaration, which, with the word "resurrection," utters that life and death are not ineluctably distributed as they are in the "old man." Faith publicly acknowledges that the subjective apparatus commanded by the law is not the only possible one. But it becomes apparent that faith, confessing the resurrection of one man, merely declares a *possibility* for everyone. That a new assemblage of life and death is possible is borne out by resurrection, and this is what must first be declared. But this conviction leaves the universalization of the "new man" in suspense and says nothing as to the content of the reconciliation between living thought and action. Faith says: We *can* escape powerlessness and rediscover that from which the law separated us. Faith prescribes a new possibility, one that, although real in Christ, is not, as yet, in effect for everyone.

It us incumbent upon love to become law so that truth's postevental universality can continuously inscribe itself in the world, rallying subjects to the path of life. Faith is the declared thought of a possible power of thought. It is not yet this power as such. As Paul forcefully puts it, *pistis di' agapēs energoumenē*, "faith works only through love" (Gal. 5.6).

It is from this point of view that, for the Christian subject, love underwrites the return of a law that, although nonliteral, nonetheless functions as principle and consistency for the subjective energy initiated by the declaration of faith. For the new man, love is fulfillment of the break that he accomplishes with the law; it is law of the break with law, law of the truth of law. Conceived in this way, the law of love can even be supported by recollecting the content of the old law (Paul never misses an opportunity for an extension of political alliances), a content that, through love, is reduced to a single maxim that must not be carved onto stone, on pain of relapsing into death, because it is entirely subordinated to the subjectivation by faith:

Owe no one anything, except to love one another; for he who loves his neighbor has fulfilled the law. The commandments, "You shall not commit adultery, You shall not kill, You shall not steal, You shall not covet," and any other commandment, are summed up in this sentence, "You shall love your neighbor as yourself." Love does no wrong to a neighbor; therefore love is the fulfilling of the law. (Rom. 13.8–10)

This passage expresses Paul's twofold attempt:

• To reduce the multiplicity of legal prescriptions, because it is to this multiplicity of commandment that desire's moribund autonomy relates in the form of objects. A single, affirmative, and nonobjectal maxim is required. One that will not arouse the infinity of desire through the transgression of the prohibition.

• To make the maxim such that it will require faith in order to be understood.

The "love your neighbor as yourself" satisfies both conditions (and, in addition, its injunction can be found in the Old Testament, which is all to the good). This single imperative envelops no prohibition; it is pure affirmation. And it requires faith, because *prior to the Resurrection, the subject, having been given up to death, has no good reason to love himself.*

Paul is in no way a theoretician of oblatory love, through which one would forget oneself in devotion to the Other. This false love, which claims that the subject annihilates himself in a direct relation to the transcendence of the Other, is nothing more than narcissistic pretension. It falls under the fourth discourse, that of the private, unspeakable word. Paul knows full well that genuine love exists only to the extent that one first be capable of loving oneself. But this relation of love the subject bears to himself is never anything but love of that living truth that institutes the subject who declares it. Thus, love is under the authority of the event and its subjectivation in faith, since only the event allows the subject to be something other than a dead Self, which it is impossible to love.

Thus, the new faith consists in deploying the power of self-love in the direction of others, addressing it to everyone, in a way made possible by subjectivation (conviction). *Love is precisely what faith is capable of.*

I call this universal power of subjectivation an evental fidelity, and it is correct to say that fidelity is the law of a truth. In Paul's thought, love is precisely fidelity to the Christ-event, in accordance with a power that *addresses* the love of self universally. Love is what makes of thought a power, which is why love alone, and not faith, bears the *force* of salvation.

What we have here is:

> *Theorem 6.* What grants power to a truth, and determines subjective fidelity, is the universal address of the relation to self instituted by the event, and not this relation itself.

This could be called the theorem of the militant. No truth is ever solitary, or particular.

To understand the Pauline version of the theorem of the militant, it is useful to proceed on the basis of two apparently contradictory statements.

Paul seems to assign salvation exclusively to faith. This is even what his thought is often reduced to. For instance (but the theme recurs throughout the epistles):

Yet knowing that a man is not justified by works of the law but through faith in Jesus Christ, even we have believed in Christ Jesus, in order to be justified by faith in Christ, and not by works of the law, because by works of the law shall no one be justified. (Gal. 2.16)

But Paul, with equal energy, assigns salvation to love alone, even going so far as to maintain that faith without love is no more than hollow subjectivism. Thus:

If I speak in the tongues of men and angels, but have not love, I am a noisy gong or a clanging cymbal. And if I have prophetic powers, and understand all mysteries and all knowledge, and if I have all faith, so as to remove mountains, but have not love, I am nothing. If I give away all I have, and if I deliver my body to be burned, but have not love, I gain nothing. (Cor. I.13.1–3)

And when it comes to classifying the three major subjective operations proper to the new man—faith, love, and charity, or rather, conviction, certainty, and love—it is to love, without hesitation, that Paul assigns pride of place: "These three abide, faith, hope, love; but the greatest of these is love" (Cor. I.13.13).

On the one hand, the evental declaration founds the subject; on the other, without love, without fidelity, that declaration is useless. Let us say that a subjectivation that does not discover the resource of power proper to its universal address misses the truth for whose sudden emergence it seemed to be the sole witness.

In the case of the preeminence of love, which alone effectuates the unity of thought and action in the world, it is necessary to pay careful attention to Paul's lexicon, which is always extremely precise. When it is a question of subjectivation through faith, Paul speaks not of salvation (*sōtēria*), but of justification (*dikaiōma*). It is true that a man is "justified by faith" (Rom. 3.28), but it is no less true that he is saved only by love. We should recall in passing that if "justification" retains, at its root, the legal motif of justice, salvation means, quite simply, "liberation." Thus, subjectivation creates, according to the possibility indicated by the resurrection of a single man, the just space of a liberation; but only love, which implies the universality of address, effectuates this liberation. Love alone is the life of truth, the pleasure of truth. As Paul says: "Love . . . rejoices in the truth [*hē agapē . . . sunkairei tēi alētheiai*]" (Cor. I.13.6).

Paul has the intuition that every subject is the articulation of a subjectivation and a consistency. This also means there is no instantaneous salvation; grace itself is no more than the indication of a possibility. The subject has to be given in his labor, and not only in his sudden emergence. "Love" is the name of that labor. Truth for Paul is never anything but "faith working through love" (Gal. 5.6).

This is the same as saying that the impetus of a truth, what makes it exist in the world, is identical to its universality, whose subjective form, under the Pauline name of love, consists in its tirelessly addressing itself to all the others, Greeks and Jews, men and women, free men and slaves. Whence the consequence that "we have no power against the truth [*ou dunametha kata tēs alētheias*], but only for the truth [*huper tēs alētheias*]" (Cor. II.13.8).

> *Theorem 7.* The subjective process of a truth is one and the same thing as the love of that truth. And the militant real of that love is the universal address of what constitutes it. The materiality of universalism is the militant dimension of every truth.

9

Hope

Paul claims that "These three abide, faith [*pistis*], hope [*elpis*], love [*agapē*, charity]" (Cor. I.13.13). We have clarified the subjective correlation between faith and love. What about hope?

With Paul and his successors, hope is described as pertaining to justice. Faith allows one to have hope in justice. Thus, in Romans 10.10: "For man believes with his heart and so obtains justice."

But what kind of justice are we talking about? Does Paul mean that the hope in justice is the hope in a judgment, the Last Judgment? That would be hope in an event to come, one that would separate the condemned from the saved. Justice would be done, and it is in this final tribunal of truth that hope would put its trust.

Against this classic judicial eschatology, Paul seems instead to characterize hope as a simple imperative of continuation, a principle of tenacity, of obstinacy. In Thessalonians I, faith is compared to striving (*ergon*), and love to grueling work, to the laborious, the troublesome. Hope, for its part, pertains to endurance, to perseverance, to patience; it is the subjectivity proper to the continuation of the subjective process.

Faith would be the opening to the true; love, the universalizing effectiveness of its trajectory; hope, lastly, a maxim enjoining us to persevere in this trajectory.

How is the idea of judgment, of justice, finally rendered, connected to that of perseverance, to that of the imperative "You must go on"? If perseverance is privileged, one obtains a subjective figure that is entirely disinterested, except for its being a coworker for a truth. Both tendencies have a long history whose political resonances are still being felt. The question is always one of knowing to what one ascribes the militant energy of an anonymous subject.

If final retribution is privileged, the subject is aligned once more with the object. Alternatively, if hope is the principle of perseverance, one remains within the realm of the purely subjective. Christianity has advanced under cover of this tension, almost invariably privileging retribution, which is more popular in the eyes of the Church, just as ordinary syndicalism points to people's protests the better to be wary of their "unrealistic" political enthusiasms.

The problem is that of knowing what relation hope has to power. Does it reinforce power *from outside*, according to what one hopes for? Is there an event to come that will reward us for our painstaking declaration of the event that constitutes us? Hope then becomes an eventual connection; it deploys the subject in the interval between two events, and the subject relies on his hope in the second in order to sustain his faith in the first.

The classic objectivating doctrine says that the final Judgment will legitimate believers by punishing unbelievers. Justice then becomes a dividing up, as seen in those great paintings by Tintoretto or Michelangelo, visually luxuriating in the contrast between the luminous ascension of the rewarded militants and the dark fall of the stricken evildoers.

Hell has always enjoyed greater artistic and public success than heaven, because what the subject requires, according to this version of hope, is the idea that the evildoer will be punished. The legitimation of faith and love through hope is then entirely negative. Hope is traversed by the hatred of others, by resentment. But thus conceived, hope seems somewhat incompatible with that reconciliation of thought and power in the universal that Paul names love.

In fact, one does not find the judicial, objective conception of hope in Paul. Certainly, because he is a violent, grudge-bearing man (for how could the path of death not persist in dividing the subject?), there are occasions in which he lets it be understood that the evildoers—which is to say, primarily his political opponents in the construction of Christian cells—will not be particularly well treated. Similarly, like any Jew living in the early days of the empire, he occasionally allows himself to imagine that our days are numbered, that the end of the world will soon be upon us: "Besides this you know what hour it is, how it is full time now for you to wake from sleep. For salvation is nearer to us now than when we first believed; the night is far gone, the day is at hand. Let us then cast off the works of darkness and put on the armor of light" (Rom. 13.11). But there are very few concessions to this aggressive, apocalyptic atmosphere in Paul. Still less does he tether hope to the satisfaction that feeds on the punishment of the wicked.

For universalism is Paul's passion, and it is not by chance that he was named the "apostle of the nations." His clearest conviction is that the evental figure of the Resurrection exceeds its real, contingent site, which is the community of believers such as it exists at the moment. The work of love is still before us; the empire is vast. This man, or this people, who are to all appearances impious and ignorant, must primarily be seen as those to whom the militant must bring the Good News. Paul's universalism will not allow the content of hope to be a privilege accorded to the faithful who happen to be living now. It is inappropriate to make distributive justice the referent for hope.

Ultimately, in Paul's eyes, hope is not hope in an objective victory. On the contrary, it is subjective victory that produces hope. We must try to understand this difficult text, whose implications are far-reaching for whoever is the militant of a truth: "And we rejoice in our hope of sharing the glory of God. More than that, we rejoice in our sufferings, knowing that suffering produces patience, and patience produces enduring fidelity, and enduring fidelity produces hope, and hope does not disappoint" (Rom. 5.2).

The subjective dimension named "hope" is the ordeal that has been overcome, not that in the name of which it has been overcome. Hope is "enduring fidelity," tenacity of love through the ordeal, and in no way vision of a reward or punishment. Hope is the subjectivity of a victorious fidelity, fidelity to fidelity, and not the representation of its future outcome.

Hope indicates the real of fidelity in the ordeal of its exercise, here and now. This is how the enigmatic expression "hope does not disappoint" should be understood. We will compare it to the statement by La-can, for whom "anxiety is what does not disappoint," precisely on ac-count of its being charged with the real, of the excess of the real from which it results. One could say that hope is not the imaginary of an ideal justice dispensed at last, but what accompanies the patience of truth, or the practical universality of love, through the ordeal of the real.

If Paul—quite apart from his general opposition to the idea that faith has a "wage"—cannot subordinate hope to the imaginary of a retri-bution, it is because resurrection has no meaning independently of the universal character of its operation. As soon as it is a question of contin-gency and grace, all fixing of divisions or distributions is forbidden: "A single act of righteousness leads to acquittal and life for all men" (Rom. 5.18). The "all men" returns without exception: "For as in Adam all die, so also in Christ shall all be made alive" (Cor. I.15.22). There is no place here for vengeance and resentment. Hell, the roasting spit of enemies, holds no interest for Paul.

Nonetheless, *one* enemy is identifiable, and its name is death. But it is a generic name, one that is applicable to a path of thought. Of this en-emy, Paul, on rare occasions, speaks in the future tense: "The last enemy who will be destroyed is death" (Cor. I.15.26). The justice that is in ques-tion in hope can doubtless be described as the death of death. But it is a question of undertaking the defeat of the subjective figure of death as of now. Justice is copresent with love's universal address and does not lead to any judicial separation between the saved and the condemned. Hope, as confidence in the fidelity of the militant, affirms instead that every vic-tory is in reality a victory for everyone. Hope is the subjective modality of a victory of the universal: "And so all Israel will be saved" (Rom. 11.26).

Just as love is the general power of self-love turned toward everyone as the construction of living thought, similarly, hope weaves the subjec-tivity of salvation, of the unity of thought and power, as a universality that is present in each ordeal, in each victory. Each victory won, however localized, is universal.

For Paul, it is of utmost importance to declare that I am justified only insofar as everyone is. Of course, hope concerns me. But this means that I identify myself in my singularity as subject of the economy of sal-vation only insofar as this economy is universal.

Hope indicates that I can persevere in love only because love inaugurates the concrete universality of the true, and this universality subsumes me, affects me in return. This is the strong sense of the statement "If I . . . have not love, I am nothing" (Cor. I.13.2). For Paul, universality mediates identity. It is the "for all" that allows me to be counted as one. Wherein we rediscover a major Pauline principle: the One is inaccessible without the "for all." What designates and verifies my participation in salvation—from the moment I become a patient worker for the universality of the true—is called hope. From this point of view, hope has nothing to do with the future. It is a figure of the present subject, who is affected in return by the universality for which he works.

Theorem 8. Where the imperative of his own continuation is concerned, the subject supports himself through the fact that the taking-place of the truth constituting him is universal and thereby effectively concerns him. There is singularity only insofar as there is universality. Failing that, there is, outside of truth, only particularity.

10

Universality and the Traversal
of Differences

That hope is the pure patience of the subject, the inclusion of self in the universality of the address, in no way implies that differences should be ignored or dismissed. For although it is true, so far as what the event constitutes is concerned, that there is "neither Greek nor Jew," *the fact is* that there are Greeks and Jews. That every truth procedure collapses differences, infinitely deploying a purely generic multiplicity, does not permit us to lose sight of the fact that, in the situation (call it: the world), *there are differences.* One can even maintain that there is nothing else.

The ontology underlying Paul's preaching valorizes nonbeings against beings, or rather, it establishes that, for the subject of a truth, what exists is generally held by established discourses to be nonexistent, while the beings validated by these discourses are, for the subject, nonexistent. Nevertheless, these fictitious beings, these opinions, customs, differences, are that to which universality is addressed; that toward which love is directed; finally, that which must be traversed in order for universality itself to be constructed, or for the genericity (*généricité*) of the true to be *immanently* deployed. Any other attitude would return truth, not to the work of love (which is unity of thought and power), but to the enclosure of that mystical fourth discourse of illumination, which Paul, who intends to ensure the transmission of the Good News throughout the entire extent of the empire, does not want to see monopolizing and sterilizing the event.

This is the reason why Paul, apostle of the nations, not only refuses to stigmatize differences and customs, but also undertakes to accommodate them so that the process of their subjective disqualification might pass through them, within them. It is in fact the search for new differences, new particularities to which the universal might be *exposed*, that leads Paul beyond the evental site properly speaking (the Jewish site) and encourages him to displace the experience historically, geographically, ontologically. Whence a highly characteristic militant tonality, combining the appropriation of particularities with the immutability of principles, the empirical existence of differences with their essential nonexistence, according to a succession of problems requiring resolution, rather than through an amorphous synthesis. The text is charged with a remarkable intensity:

> For though I am free from all men, I have made myself a slave to all, that I might win the more. To the Jews I became as a Jew, in order to win the Jews; to those under the law, I became as one under the law—though not being myself under the law—that I might win those under the law. To those outside the law I became as one outside the law—not being without law toward God but under the law of Christ—that I might win those outside the law. To the weak I became weak, that I might win the weak. I have become all things to all men. (Cor. I.9.19–22)

This is not an opportunist text, but an instance of what Chinese communists will call "the mass line," pushed to its ultimate expression in "serving the people." It consists in supposing that, whatever people's opinions and customs, once gripped by a truth's postevental work, their thought becomes capable of traversing and transcending those opinions and customs without having to give up the differences that allow them to recognize themselves in the world.

But in order for people to become gripped by truth, it is imperative that universality not present itself under the aspect of a particularity. Differences can be transcended only if benevolence with regard to customs and opinions presents itself as *an indifference that tolerates differences*, one whose sole material test lies, as Paul says, in being able and knowing how to practice them oneself. Whence Paul's extreme wariness with regard to every rule, every rite, that would assume the form of universalist militantism by making of it a bearer of differences and particularities in turn.

Of course, the faithful belonging to small Christian cells incessantly ask Paul what they should think about women's dress, sexual relations, permissible or prohibited foods, the calendar, astrology, and so forth. For it is in the nature of the human animal, as defined by networks of differences, to love asking questions of this type and even to think that they alone are really important. Confronted with this barrage of problems far removed from what, for him, identifies the Christian subject, Paul displays an inflexible impatience: "If anyone is disposed to be contentious, we do not recognize that practice" (Cor. I.11.16). It is in fact of utmost importance for the destiny of universalist labor that the latter be withdrawn from conflicts of opinion and confrontations between customary differences. The fundamental maxim is *mē eis diakriseis dialogismōn,* "do not argue about opinions" (Rom. 14.1).

This injunction is all the more striking in that *diakrisis* means primarily "discernment of differences." Thus, it is to the imperative not to compromise the truth procedure by entangling it in the web of opinions and differences that Paul is committed. It is certainly possible for a philosophy to argue about opinions; for Socrates, this is even what defines it. But the Christian subject is not a philosopher, and faith is neither an opinion, nor a critique of opinion. Christian militantism must traverse worldly differences indifferently and avoid all casuistry over customs.

Evidently impatient to return to the topic of resurrection, but also concerned lest he alienate his comrades, Paul takes great pains to explain that what one eats, the behavior of a servant, astrological hypotheses, and finally the fact of being Jewish, Greek, or anything else—all this can and must be envisaged as simultaneously extrinsic to the trajectory of a truth and compatible with it:

One believes he may eat anything, while the weak man eats only vegetables. Let not him who eats despise him who abstains, and let not him who abstains pass judgment on him who eats. . . . One man esteems one day as better than another, while another man esteems all days alike. Let every one be fully convinced in his own mind. (Rom. 14.2–5)

Paul goes very far in this direction, so it's very odd to see him accused of sectarian moralism. The opposite is the case, for we constantly observe him resisting demands in favor of prohibitions, rites, customs, observances. He does not hesitate to say "in truth, all things are clean [*panta kathara*]" (Rom. 14.20). And above all, he argues against moral judgment, which in his eyes is an evasion before the event's "for all": "You, why do you pass judgment on your brother? Or you, why do you despise your brother? . . . Then let us no more pass judgment on one another" (Rom. 14.10–13).

In the end, the astonishing principle proposed by this "moralist" can be formulated as: everything is permitted (*panta exestin*, Cor. I.10.23). Yes, within the order of particularity, everything is permitted. For if differences are the material of the world, it is only so that the singularity proper to the subject of truth—a singularity that is itself included in the becoming of the universal—can puncture that material. No need to presume to judge or reduce that material so far as this puncturing is concerned; indeed, quite the opposite.

That customary or particular differences are what we must *let be* from the moment we bring to bear on them the universal address and the militant consequences of faith (which is to say *only* inconsistency with respect to faith, or "whatever does not proceed from faith" [Rom. 14.23], counts as sin) can be better evaluated by considering two examples, with regard to which the accusation of sectarian moralism, or worse, has often been made against Paul: women and Jews.

It has often been claimed that Pauline teaching inaugurated the era of the Christian origins of anti-Semitism. But unless one considers that breaking with religious orthodoxy by maintaining a singular heresy from within is a form of racism—which, all things considered, is an insufferable retrospective excess—it has to be said that there is nothing remotely resembling any form of anti-Semitic statement in Paul's writings.

The accusation of "deicide," which, it is true, burdens the Jews with a crushing mythological guilt, is entirely absent from Paul's discourse, for reasons at once anecdotal and essential. Anecdotal because, in any case— we have already explained why—the historical and statist process of Jesus' putting to death, and thus the allocation of responsibilities in the matter, are of absolutely no interest to Paul, for whom only the Resurrection matters. Essential because, amply predating as it does Trinitarian theology, Paul's thought does not base itself in any way on the theme of a substantial identity of Christ and God, and there is nothing in Paul corresponding to the sacrificial motif of the crucified God.

It is rather in the Gospels, and above all in the last one, John's, that Jewish particularity is set apart, and the separation between Christians and Jews insisted upon. After the Jews' long war against Roman occupation, this probably helped elicit the goodwill of the imperial authorities, but it already serves to draw the Christian proposition away from its universal destination, paving the way for the differentiating regime of exceptions and exclusions.

We find nothing of the sort in Paul. His relation to Jewish particularity is essentially positive. Conscious of the extent to which the eventual site remains, genealogically and ontologically, within the heritage of biblical monotheism, he even goes so far, when designating the universality of the address, as to accord Jews a kind of priority. For instance, "Glory and honor and peace for every one who does good, the Jew first and also the Greek" (Rom. 2.10).

"For the Jew first [*Ioudaiōi prōton*]": this is precisely what marks the Jewish difference's pride of place in the movement traversing *all* differences so that the universal can be constructed. This is why Paul not only considers the necessity of making oneself "a Jew among Jews" obvious, but also vigorously invokes his Jewishness so as to establish that the Jews are included in the universality of the Announcement: "I ask then, has God rejected his people? By no means! I myself am an Israelite, a descendant of Abraham, a member of the tribe of Benjamin. God has not rejected his people, whom he foreknew" (Rom. 11.1).

Of course, Paul fights against all those who would submit postevental universality to Jewish particularity. He fervently hopes to be "delivered from the unbelievers in Judea" (Rom. 15.31). It is the least that could be expected from him who identifies his faith only in being affected by the collapse of customary and communitarian differences. But in no way is it a question of judging the Jews as such, all the less so because, ultimately, Paul's conviction, unlike John's, is that "all Israel will be saved" (Rom. 11.26).

The truth is that Paul mobilizes the new discourse in a constant, subtle strategy of displacement relative to Jewish discourse. We have already remarked that references to the Old Testament are as abundant in Paul's texts as those to the sayings of Christ are absent. The task Paul sets for himself is obviously not that of abolishing Jewish particularity, which he constantly acknowledges as the event's principle of historicity, but that of animating it internally by everything of which it is capable relative to the new discourse, and hence the new subject. For Paul, being Jewish in general, and the Book in particular, *can and must be resubjectivated.*

This operation finds a basis in the opposition between the figure of Moses and that of Abraham. Paul does not much like Moses, man of the letter and the law. By contrast, he readily identifies with Abraham for two very powerful reasons, both contained in a passage from the epistle to the Galatians (3.6): "Thus Abraham 'believed God and it was reckoned to him as righteousness.' So you see that it is men of faith who are the sons of Abraham. And the scripture, foreseeing that God would justify the Gentiles by faith, preached the gospel beforehand to Abraham, saying, 'In you shall all the nations be blessed.' So then, those who are men of faith are blessed with Abraham, who had faith."

One sees here that Abraham is decisive for Paul. First because he was elected by God solely by virtue of his faith, before the law (which was engraved for Moses, Paul notes, "four hundred and thirty years later"); second because the promise that accompanies his election pertains to "all the nations," rather than to Jewish descendants alone. Abraham thereby anticipates what could be called a universalism of the Jewish site; in other words, he anticipates Paul. A Jew among Jews, and proud of it, Paul only wishes to remind us that it is absurd to believe oneself a proprietor of God, and that an event wherein what is at issue is life's triumph over death, regardless of the communitarian forms assumed by one or the other, activates the "for all" through which the One of genuine monotheism sustains itself. This is a reminder in which, once again, the Book plays a part in subjectivation: "He has called us not from the Jews only but also from the Gentiles. As indeed he says in Hosea, 'Those who were not my people I will call my people, and her who was not beloved I will call my beloved'" (Rom. 9.24).

Where women are concerned, it is equally false, albeit frequently maintained, that Paul is the founder of a Christian misogyny. We shall certainly not claim that Paul, who does not want interminable quibbling over customs and opinions (this would involve compromising the transcendence of the universal through communitarian divisions), makes pronouncements about women that would seem appropriate to us today. But all things considered, there is something absurd about bringing him to trial before the tribunal of contemporary feminism. The only question worth asking is whether Paul, given the conditions of his time, is a progressive or a reactionary so far as the status of women is concerned.

One decisive factor in any case is that, in light of the fundamental statement that maintains that, in the element of faith, "there is neither male nor female," Paul clearly intends that women participate in gatherings of the faithful and be able to declare the event. As a visionary militant, Paul understood the resource in energy and expansion that such egalitarian participation would be able to mobilize. He had no wish to deprive himself of the presence at his side of "beloved Persis, who has worked hard for the Lord" (Rom. 16.12), or Julia, or Nereus's sister.

This suggests that the problem for Paul consists in reconciling—according to the circumstances—this requirement with the obvious and massive inequality affecting women in the ancient world, without the debate over this point hindering the movement of universalization.

Paul's technique then becomes one of what could be called *subsequent symmetrization*. Initially, he will concede what no one at the time is willing to call into question—for instance, the husband's authority over his wife. Whence the formulation, "The wife does not rule over her own body, but the husband does" (Cor. I.7.4). Horror! Yes, but in order for a reminder that what matters is a truth's universal becoming to be implicitly slipped into this inegalitarian maxim, it will, so to speak, be neutralized through the subsequent mention of its reversibility. For the text continues, and this continuation should really always be cited *also*: "And likewise the husband does not rule over his own body, but the wife does" (Cor. I.7.4).

Ultimately, Paul's undertaking, which, in the final analysis, it is right to consider as a progressive innovation, consists in *making universalizing egalitarianism pass through the reversibility of an inegalitarian rule*. This at once allows him to avoid irresolvable arguments over the rule (which he assumes at the outset) and to arrange the global situation so that universality *is able* to affect particularizing differences in return: in this instance, the difference between the sexes.

Whence a technique of balancing, which, as soon as women are concerned, marks all of Paul's interventions without exception. Take marriage, for example. Obviously, Paul begins with the inegalitarian rule "I give charge . . . that the wife should not separate from her husband" (Cor. I.7.10). But he immediately adds "and that the husband should not divorce his wife" (Cor. I.7.10).

Let us consider a question that, in what is known as its Islamic variant, enjoys a certain topicality: Should women cover their hair when in public? This is obviously what everyone thinks in the eastern world in which the apostle is trying to start militant groups. For Paul, what is important is that a woman "prays or prophesies" (that a woman be able to "prophesy," which for Paul means publicly declare her faith, is something quite considerable). Thus, he admits that "any woman who prays or prophesies with her head unveiled dishonors her chief" (Cor. I.11.5). The argument is that women's long hair indicates something like the natural character of veiling, and that it is appropriate to emphasize this natural veil with an artificial sign that ultimately pays witness to an acceptance of the difference between the sexes. As Paul says, for a woman, true shame consists in being shorn, and this is the one and only reason why, being summoned to declaration, she must veil herself in order to show that the universality of this declaration *includes women who confirm that they are women.* It is the power of the universal over difference as difference that is at issue here.

It will be objected that this constraint applies solely to women, and hence that it is flagrantly unequal. But such is not the case, on account of the subsequent symmetrization. For Paul is careful to specify that "any man who prays or prophesies with his head covered dishonors his chief" (Cor. I.11.4), and that it is as shameful for a man to have long hair as it is for a woman to have short hair. The necessity of traversing and testifying to the difference between the sexes *in order for it* to become indifferent in the universality of the declaration culminates in symmetrical, rather than unilateral, constraints within the contingent realm of customs.

Perhaps echoing a hierarchical vision of the world that was ubiquitous at the time, and whose Roman version was the cult of the emperor,

Paul does declare that "the chief of every man is Christ, the chief of a woman is her husband, and the chief of Christ is God" (Cor. I.11.3). Moreover, it is precisely the ambiguity of the word *kephalē* (still audible in the ancient word "chief") that allows him to move from this theologico-cosmic disquisition to an examination of the perilous question of the women's veil. As expected, the basis is provided by the narrative in Genesis: "For man was not made from woman, but woman from man" (8). The question seems settled: Paul proposes a solid religious basis for the subjugation of women. Well actually, not at all. Three lines further down, a vigorous "nevertheless" (*plēn*) introduces the subsequent symmetrization, which, opportunely reminding us that every man is born of a woman, leads the whole of this inegalitarian edifice back to an essential equality: "Nevertheless, in the Lord woman is not independent of man, nor man of woman; for as woman was made from man, so man is now born of woman" (Cor. I.11.11).

Thus, Paul remains faithful to his twofold conviction. With regard to what has happened to us, to what we subjectivate through a public declaration (faith), to what we universalize through a fidelity (love), and with which we identify our subjective consistency in time (hope), differences are indifferent, and the universality of the true collapses them. With regard to the world in which truth proceeds, universality must expose itself to all differences and show, through the ordeal of their division, that they are capable of welcoming the truth that traverses them. What matters, man or woman, Jew or Greek, slave or free man, is that differences *carry the universal that happens to them like a grace.* Inversely, only by recognizing in differences their capacity for carrying the universal that comes upon them can the universal itself verify its own reality: "If even lifeless instruments, such as the flute or the harp, do not give distinct notes, how will anyone know what is being played on the flute or the harp?" (Cor. I.14.7).

Differences, like instrumental tones, provide us with the recognizable univocity that makes up the melody of the True.

11

In Conclusion

We gave this book the subtitle *The Foundation of Universalism*. It is, of course, an excessive title. Real universalism is already entirely present in this or that theorem of Archimedes, in certain political practices of the Greeks, in a tragedy of Sophocles, or in the amorous intensity to which the poems of Sappho bear witness. It is just as present in the Psalms, or, inverted into nihilism, in the lamentations of Ecclesiastes.

Nevertheless, there occurs with Paul, on this very issue, a powerful break, one that is still illegible in the teaching of Jesus, insofar we have access to it. Only this break illuminates the immense echo of the Christian foundation.

The difficulty for us is that this break has no bearing on the explicit content of the doctrine. The Resurrection, after all, is just a mythological assertion. The claim "there is a limitless succession of prime numbers" possesses an indubitable universality. The claim "Christ is resurrected" is as though subtracted from the opposition between the universal and the particular, because it is a narrative statement that we cannot assume to be historical.

In reality, the Pauline break has a bearing upon the formal conditions and the inevitable consequences of a consciousness-of-truth rooted in a pure event, detached from every objectivist assignation to the particular laws of a world or society yet concretely destined to become inscribed within a world and within a society. What Paul must be given exclusive credit for establishing is that the fidelity to such an event exists only through the termination of communitarian particularisms and the determination of a subject-of-truth who indistinguishes the One and the "for all." Thus, unlike effective truth procedures (science, art, politics, love), the Pauline break does not base itself upon the production of a universal. Its bearing, in a mythological context implacably reduced to a single point, a single statement (Christ is resurrected), pertains rather to the laws of universality in general. This is why it can be called a *theoretical* break, it being understood that in this instance "theoretical" is not being opposed to "practical," but to real. Paul is a founder, in that he is one of the very first theoreticians of the universal.

A second difficulty is then that Paul could be identified as a philosopher. I have myself maintained that what is proper to philosophy is not the production of universal truths, but rather the organization of their synthetic reception by forging and reformulating the category of Truth. Auguste Comte defined the philosopher as one who "specialized in generalities." Is not Paul someone who specializes in the general categories of all universalism?

We will suspend this objection by claiming that Paul is not a philosopher precisely because he assigns his thought to a singular event, rather than a set of conceptual generalities. That this singular event is of the order of a fable prohibits Paul from being an artist, or a scientist, or a revolutionary of the State, but also prohibits all access to philosophical subjectivity, which either subordinates itself to conceptual foundation or auto-foundation, or places itself under the condition of *real* truth procedures. For Paul, the truth event repudiates philosophical Truth, while for us the fictitious dimension of this event repudiates its pretension to real truth.

Accordingly, we must say: *Paul is an antiphilosophical theoretician of universality.* That the event (or pure act) invoked by antiphilosophers is fictitious does not present a problem. It is equally so in Pascal (it is the same as Paul's), or in Nietzsche (Nietzsche's "grand politics" did not break the history of the world in two; it was Nietzsche who was broken).

Antiphilosopher of genius, Paul warns the philosopher that the conditions for the universal cannot be conceptual, either in origin, or in destination.

So far as the origin is concerned, it is necessary that an event, which is a sort of grace supernumerary to every particularity, be what one proceeds from in order to cast off differences.

So far as the destination is concerned, it can be neither predicative nor judicial. There is no authority before which the result of a truth procedure could be brought to trial. A truth never appertains to Critique. It is supported only by itself and is the correlate of a new type of subject, neither transcendental nor substantial, entirely defined as militant of the truth in question.

This is why, as Paul testifies in exemplary fashion, universalism, which is an absolute (nonrelative) subjective production, indistinguishes saying and doing, thought and power. Thought becomes universal only by addressing itself to all others, and it effectuates itself as power through this address. But the moment all, including the solitary militant, are counted according to the universal, it follows that what takes place is the subsumption of the Other by the Same. Paul demonstrates in detail how a universal thought, proceeding on the basis of the worldly proliferation of alterities (the Jew, the Greek, women, men, slaves, free men, and so on), *produces* a Sameness and an Equality (there is no longer either Jew, or Greek, and so on). The production of equality and the casting off, in thought, of differences are the material signs of the universal.

Against universalism conceived of as production of the Same, it has recently been claimed that the latter found its emblem, if not its culmination, in the death camps, where everyone, having been reduced to a body on the verge of death, was absolutely equal to everyone else. This "argument" is fraudulent, for two major reasons. The first is that, in reading Primo Levi or Shalamov, one sees that, on the contrary, the death camp produces exorbitant differences at every instant, that it turns the slightest fragment of reality into an absolute difference between life and death, and this incessant differentiation of the minute is a torture. The second, more directly relevant to Paul, is that one of the necessary conditions of thought as power (which, let us remind ourselves, is love) consists in he who is a militant of the truth identifying himself, as well as everyone else, on the basis of the universal. *The production of the Same is itself internal to the law of the Same.* But the Nazis' production of exterminatory abattoirs obeyed the opposite principle: the "meaning" proper to the mass production of Jewish corpses was that of delimiting the existence of the master race as absolute difference. The address to the other of the "as oneself" (love the other as yourself) was what the Nazis wanted to abolish. The German Aryan's "as oneself" was precisely what could not be projected anywhere, a closed substance, continuously driven to verify its own closure, both in and outside itself, through carnage.

Paul's maxim, which is that of the dissolution of the universalizing subject's identity in the universal, makes of the Same that which must be achieved, even if it includes, when necessary, altering our own alterity.

For the subject, this subjective logic culminates in an indifference to secular nominations, to whatever allocates predicates and hierarchical values to particular subsets. Hope outstrips these nominations. The epistle to the Philippians (2.9) speaks of Christ as "the name which is above every name." It is always to such names, rather than to the closed names proper to particular languages and sealed entities, that the subject of a truth lays claim. All true names are "above every name." They let themselves be inflected and declared, just as mathematical symbolism does, in every language, according to every custom, and through the traversal of all differences.

Every name from which a truth proceeds is a name from before the Tower of Babel. But it has to circulate in the tower.

Paul, we have insisted, is not a dialectician. The universal is not the negation of particularity. It is the measured advance across a distance relative to perpetually subsisting particularity. Every particularity is a conformation, a conformism. It is a question of maintaining a nonconformity with regard to that which is always conforming us. Thought is subjected to the ordeal of conformity, and only the universal, through an uninterrupted labor, an inventive traversal, relieves it. As Paul magnificently puts it, "Do not be conformed to the present century, but be transformed by the renewal of your thought [*nous* here, and not *pneuma*, so that it is better not to translate it as "spirit"]" (Rom. 12.2).

Far from fleeing from the century, one must live with it, but without letting oneself be shaped, conformed. It is the subject, rather than the century, who, under the injunction of his faith, must be transformed. And the key to this transformation, this "renewal," lies in thought.

Paul says to us: it is always possible for a nonconformist thought to think in the century. This is what a subject is. It is he who maintains the universal, not conformity.

Only what is in immanent exception is universal.

But if everything depends on an event, must we wait? Certainly not. Many events, even very distant ones, still require us to be faithful to them. Thought does not wait, and it has never exhausted its reserve of power, unless it be for him who succumbs to the profound desire to conform, which is the path of death.

Besides, waiting is pointless, for it is of the essence of the event not to be preceded by any sign, and to catch us unawares with its grace, regardless of our vigilance.

In Zarathustra's dialogue with the fire-dog, Nietzsche says that true events arrive on doves' feet, that they surprise us in the moment of greatest silence. On this point, as on many others, he should have acknowledged his debt to that same Paul upon whom he pours out his scorn. First epistle to the Thessalonians (5.2): "The day of the Lord will come like a thief in the night."

Cultural Memory | *in the Present*

Alain Badiou, *Saint Paul: The Foundation of Universalism*

Bernard Faure, *Double Exposure: Cutting Across Buddhist and Western Discourses*

Stanley Cavell, *Emerson's Transcendental Etudes*

Stuart McLean, *The Event and Its Terrors: Ireland, Famine, Modernity*

Beate Rössler, ed., *Privacies*

Gil Anidjar, *The Jew, the Arab: A History of the Enemy*

Jonathan Culler and Kevin Lamb, eds., *Just Being Difficult? Academic Writing in the Public Arena*

Jean-Luc Nancy, *A Finite Thinking*, edited by Simon Sparks

Theodor W. Adorno, *Can One Live after Auschwitz? A Philosophical Reader*, edited by Rolf Tiedemann

Patricia Pisters, *The Matrix of Visual Culture: Working with Deleuze in Film Theory*

Talal Asad, *Formations of the Secular: Christianity, Islam, Modernity*

Dorothea von Mücke, *The Rise of the Fantastic Tale*

Marc Redfield, *The Politics of Aesthetics: Nationalism, Gender, Romanticism*

Emmanuel Levinas, *On Escape*

F. R. Ankersmit, *Political Representation*

Elissa Marder, *Dead Time: Temporal Disorders in the Wake of Modernity (Baudelaire and Flaubert)*

Reinhart Koselleck, *The Practice of Conceptual History: Timing History, Spacing Concepts*

Niklas Luhmann, *The Reality of the Mass Media*

Hubert Damisch, *A Childhood Memory by Piero della Francesca*

Hubert Damisch, *A Theory of /Cloud/: Toward a History of Painting*

Jean-Luc Nancy, *The Speculative Remark (One of Hegel's Bons Mots)*

Jean-François Lyotard, *Soundproof Room: Malraux's Anti-Aesthetics*

Jan Patočka, *Plato and Europe*

Hubert Damisch, *Skyline: The Narcissistic City*

Isabel Hoving, *In Praise of New Travelers: Reading Caribbean Migrant Women Writers*

Richard Rand, ed., *Futures: Of Jacques Derrida*

William Rasch, *Niklas Luhmann's Modernity: The Paradoxes of Differentiation*

Jacques Derrida and Anne Dufourmantelle, *Of Hospitality*

Jean-François Lyotard, *The Confession of Augustine*

Kaja Silverman, *World Spectators*

Samuel Weber, *Institution and Interpretation*, expanded edition

Jeffrey S. Librett, *The Rhetoric of Cultural Dialogue: Jews and Germans in the Epoch of Emancipation*

Ulrich Baer, *Remnants of Song: Trauma and the Experience of Modernity in Charles Baudelaire and Paul Celan*

Samuel C. Wheeler III, *Deconstruction as Analytic Philosophy*